JHAKE·
JHÆFTE
& OTHER PLAYJ

SHAKE-SHAFTE

& OTHER PLAYS

ROWAN WILLIAMS

FOREWORD BY
JAY PARINI

SL/.NT
BOOKS

SHAKESHAFTE & OTHER PLAYS

Slant Books
P.O. Box 60295
Seattle, WA 98160

www.slantbooks.com

HARDCOVER ISBN: 978-1-63982-103-7
PAPERBACK ISBN: 978-1-63982-102-0
EBOOK ISBN: 978-1-63982-104-4

Cataloguing-in-Publication data:

Names: Williams, Rowan

Title: Shakeshafte & other plays. / Rowan Williams.

Description: Seattle, WA: Slant, 2021.

Identifiers: ISBN 978-1-63982-103-7 (hardcover) | ISBN 978-1-63982-102-0 (paperback) | ISBN 978-1-63982-104-4 (ebook)

Subjects: LCSH: Shakespeare, William, 1564-1616 -- Drama | Campion, Edmund, -- Saint, -- 1540-1581 | Lazarus, -- of Bethany, Saint -- Fiction.

Classification: PR6123 .I43293 S5 2021. (paperback) | PR6123 .I43293 S5 2021. (ebook)

Library of Congress Control Number: 2021946665.

Contents

Foreword

ONE LOOKS BACK at the writings of Rowan Williams, formerly the Archbishop of Canterbury (2002–2012), with amazement and gratitude. He's a compulsively readable and persuasive theologian and Christian apologist, one whose early work was strongly influenced by the bracing mysticism of Eastern Orthodoxy (his doctoral research being a study of the Russian theologian Vladimir Nikolayevich Lossky). Among his most arresting works in a theological vein are *The Wound of Knowledge* (1979), a survey of Christian spirituality from the New Testament through St. John of the Cross, and *Silence and Honey Cakes* (2003), a splendid reading of the desert monastics of the fourth century, who wrote movingly about finding Christ in community. But this scarcely begins to tell the story of Williams as a theologian – a journey that, to a degree, culminates in *Christ the Heart of Creation* (2018), a beautifully argued meditation on how over two millennia Christians have engaged with the paradoxes of the Christ figure and the relations between God and creation itself.

Williams is also a gifted poet and literary critic, prolific in both genres. His poems reflect his deep reading in poetry, in history, his love of art and music, and his alertness to landscapes (especially the Welsh landscape of his childhood), where nature and spirit live in easy correspondence. His evocative and sensuous language offers a rich experience. And as a literary critic, especially in his luminous studies of Dostoevsky (2008) and C. S. Lewis (2012), he's an astute, responsive, and helpful reader – always at the service of the text, which he inhabits with an almost uncanny ability to lose himself in a writer's world, with an enduring interest in metaphor itself as the heart of communication – a topic he explored in tantalizing detail in his Gifford Lectures, published as *The Edge of Words* (2014).

All of which brings us to Shakespeare, the subject of his first play in *Shakeshafte and Other Plays*. In his youth, Williams entertained visions of the stage, acting in several plays. In a 2014 interview with *The Guardian*, he revealed his abiding love of the Bard, calling *The Winter's Tale* "one of the most linguistically dense, emotionally demanding, and spiritually rich of all the plays." He said that he found the long-standing arguments about Shakespeare's Roman Catholic leanings of more than passing interest:

> Shakespeare knows exactly where he does, and doesn't, want to go, in matters of church and state. He deliberately puts some of his plays right outside the Christian, Tudor/Jacobean framework. For instance, *King Lear* takes place in a pre-Christian Britain. Again, some people argue that *Cymbeline* is about a rupture with Rome, leading to a reconciliation. I think Shakespeare did have a recusant Catholic background. My own hunch is that he didn't go to church much.

In this same interview he refers to the first play in this collection, *Shakeshafte*.

Here he imagines a dialogue between young Will and the legendary Jesuit martyr, Edmund Campion. "We know they both stayed at the same house in Lancashire," he says. "I found this a wonderful idea to play with: what might a Jesuit martyr and Shakespeare have said to each other?"

This play is more than simply an imaginary conversation between two major figures. It's a striking portrait of Catholic life in Elizabethan England, when a secret papist might be exposed, leading to partial hanging, castration, disembowelment, and beheading – the hideous fate that actually befell Campion in 1581. The actual details of these executions terrified all Catholics in Elizabeth's time, and this potential fate gives a sharp edge of anxiety to the drama that unfolds in *Shakeshafte* during the winter of 1580 and the summer of 1581.

The play's setting is an opulent manor house in Lancashire, home of the wealthy Catholic Alexander Hoghton, who apparently left a bit of money to a young man called Will Shakeshafte. In Williams's drama, this man is Shakespeare himself, who by tradition once worked for a Catholic family in Lancashire as a young man. (The evidence that Shakespeare may have had Roman associations is compelling, although some scholars disagree with the notion. In any case, Williams calls this a *fantasia*, a kind of "what if" play.) The lost years of Shakespeare are, of course, an inviting gap in history, and Williams rushes into this space with relish, giving us a wise and witty young man who more than holds his own with his elders, including the mystery man who shifts about the countryside under various names, here as Edward Hastings, a priest who belongs to "the Company," which refers to the Society of Jesus, the Jesuit order.

The play, which includes a dalliance with a local lass for young Will, is provocative and entertaining, the language expressively idiomatic, the discourse bracing. In one key passage in Scene VII, for example, Will talks with Hoghton and Hastings, setting out his views of religion, which aren't exactly a model of orthodox rhetoric. "For Christ's sake, Will! You're not turning Lutheran," exclaims Alex. Here Will responds at his best: "I'm not turning anything, sir. I want to know the playbook's there, in Rome or wherever. Perhaps it's only what someone else did, what someone else said, hundreds of years ago, when they were on their own on a stage and there were no playbooks. And – you know spiders? They spin it out of themselves, don't they; they get it out of the bowels and...." He's interrupted by Hastings, who says: "What's in those bowels, though? You know your catechism. What's in any of us except lies and tales and images of who we are, that we set up and worship?"

Shakeshafte is a densely woven fabric, a play that seems utterly plausible and tantalizing as well. And it plays well against *The Flat Roof of the World*, another full-length play about a writer, although the social context of this play, and its dreamlike setting, could not be more different. David Jones, its subject, has none of Will's easy way with words. He's occasionally halting and inarticulate, at other times as eloquent as we find him in his poems.

Jones was, indeed, one of the major modernist poets of Britain, best known for *In Parenthesis* (1937), a long poem (with an admixture of prose) set during the Great War, in which Jones fought for five years – a survivor of the trenches who suffered for many decades from post-traumatic stress syndrome or "shell shock," as it was called then. Perhaps his worst time was the disastrous battle at Mametz Wood in the summer of 1916, recalled by Jones in Williams's play: "Sounds odd, bloody great explosions going off all the time, all around, but there, inside the fog, in the dawn, walking forward as if you were on cushions, walking on air, walking on the flat roof of the world."

This riveting play draws a small circle around Jones, who lived an increasingly isolated life in his later years, never well enough to follow through with marriage, barely able to function in the world. In addition to his poetry, he was a major artist, especially known for his watercolors. Soon after the war, he was drawn (as a Catholic convert) to Eric Gill, a sculptor and typeface designer associated with the Arts and Crafts Movement. Gill was a Catholic himself, and a very strange man who wrote about his sexual adventures in his diary. These included incestuous relations with his two eldest daughters – the second of whom, Petra, was briefly engaged to David Jones, who was later attracted to a vivid young actor and athlete, Valerie Wynne-Williams.

As Williams puts this cast of characters before us, the conflicts arise. Gill wants Jones to do something more serious, as an artist, than mere watercolors. "What do you think you're making when you paint one of these?" he asks the mortified Jones. "It's just...wallpaper for some capitalist collections; it's not a thing with a purpose." As Jones struggles in his halting relations with Petra and Valerie, he tries to make sense of a senseless world. His memories endlessly return to the trench, much as one's tongue returns to a cavity or sore in the mouth. "It all comes back to that, though, doesn't it?" he says to Petra in Scene IV. "A man hung up in public, dying. Don't get me wrong, don't think I'm getting a Christ-complex. It's just that I suppose he hangs up there because that's where we all are, one way or another. Dying, surviving. Waiting."

Williams is, at core, a Christian playwright, interested in questions of sacrifice, even self-sacrifice. He shows not the slightest fear in approaching the oddities of Gill, the torment of his daughter, or the frustrations of Valerie, who says in rejecting him for another man: "If you'd really wanted me – if you'd really wanted me and – well, I'd have.... Oh, Christ, I don't know."

The Flat Roof of the World is rooted in Jones's poetry – the title itself comes from *In Parenthesis*. And it has all the brokenness, splintered idealism, and desperate grip on the physical and spiritual realities that one associates with this poet. And yet the play is dreamlike, as characters step in and out of time, the conflicts in the poet's life coalescing in powerful clusters of confrontation and engagement. A kind of imaginative smoke seems to swirl around their legs as they lift their heads above the clouds. The total effect of this play is, finally, both devastating and hauntingly beautiful.

The final short play is *Lazarus*, a meditation in three voices. The sequence is largely a riff on the great line from the

Lazarus sequence in the 11th chapter of John's gospel: "I am the Resurrection and the Life: he that believeth in me, though he were dead, yet shall he live: And whosoever liveth and believeth in me shall never die." These words, in the King James translation, are heard "as if in church" on a grainy recording. This gives us the feeling that truth, as ever, lies at the bottom of a well, rippled over by water that obscures and distorts it. We hear the voices of a middle-aged man and woman, and a young male as each of them struggles with unique circumstances that involve death and resurrection. We're in the past, in biblical time, and the present as well. All time becomes irrelevant in the face of death and, by implication, in the reality of Resurrection thinking. Needless to say, there is much confusion on the part of our speakers, who keenly participate in the grief around and within them, and who understand on some level that Jesus wept because he saw the suffering of poor human beings, and his own humanity drew from this same depth in an act of sympathy.

This is a dramatic poem in three voices that raises some of the most profound questions that we ask about life and death. Did Lazarus really want to come back? Did his sister actually wish for this? Can we build on the process of dying, which is possibly an opening into new life? "I'm what's alive here," says the first voice near the end, in a totalizing moment. And it's this recognition that lights up this memorable little drama.

Rowan Williams invites us into three dramatic sequences that range widely, as the author's mind invariably does. And yet certain key questions play throughout: What matters to us most? What is life worth? How do we come to live in community in a way that celebrates and values who we are, perhaps who we were meant to be? It should surprise no one that Williams asks these questions, here with the kind of shimmering indirect eloquence that the drama affords.

– Jay Parini

SHAKESHAFTE

Shakeshafte

NOTE

In August 1581, Alexander Hoghton, of Lea and Hoghton Tower in Lancashire, died, after making a will in which he left bequests to a number of members of his household – a large one, as befitted one of the wealthiest men in the region, occupying an ample and spectacularly situated mansion not far from Preston.

Among the beneficiaries are Fulk Gillom (who can be traced with some likelihood as belonging to a Chester family connected with the productions of the guild plays in the city) and William Shakeshafte. In addition to receiving legacies, these two are also recommended to a neighbour, Sir Thomas Hesketh, for patronage and/or employment; the context clearly suggests that they are involved with providing entertainments for the household.

Nothing more can be learned for sure about Shakeshafte. But since Hoghton's will was first published in the nineteenth century, the similarity of the name to that of a better-known sixteenth century figure has generated a wealth of speculation. A local tradition was unearthed that Shakespeare had worked with a Catholic family in Lancashire, and John Aubrey's report that Shakespeare had in his youth been "a schoolmaster in the country" was prayed in aid. The possible

Catholic connections and sympathies of Shakespeare at various points of his life gave the thesis added plausibility for some; and Lord Strange, later Earl of Derby and an early patron of Shakespeare, had close links with Lancashire and its gentry families. More significantly, it emerged that John Cottam, schoolmaster in Stratford from 1579 to 1582, came from a family living near Hoghton Tower.

Cottam and the Hoghtons were loyal to the "old religion"; and when the Jesuit, Edmund Campion, toured the north of England in 1580-1, he stayed with different members of the Hoghton family, among other Catholic gentry households. Converted to Catholicism after a brilliant Oxford career, Campion had moved abroad to study for the priesthood, joined the Jesuits, and made a stellar reputation in Europe, spending time at the court of the Holy Roman emperor Rudolf II in Prague. He returned to England in 1580 – along with Thomas Cottam, brother of the Stratford schoolmaster, also a Jesuit priest.

At this period, Catholic missioners from abroad were regarded by Elizabeth I's government as automatically treasonous, given that the Pope in 1569 had sanctioned the removal by force or assassination of the Queen. Their reputation was much the same as that of ISIS or Al Qaeda in the present context, though very few indeed actually supported violence or rebellion. Both Cottam and Campion were executed in 1581 by the usual barbaric method of partial hanging followed by disembowelling. Campion was made a saint by the Roman Catholic Church in 1970.

So there is a strong likelihood that Campion was either at Hoghton Tower or at Alexander Hoghton's other residence at Lea during some period in 1580-1. Whoever William Shakeshafte really was may well have been there at the same time. Scholars differ very sharply about the likelihood of the identification of Shakeshafte with the young man from Stratford; several leading Shakespearean experts such as Katherine Duncan-Jones and Jonathan Bate believe that the

Lancashire connection is wholly discredited, and a plausible local candidate for identification with Shakeshafte has been traced; but others still consider it a possibility, given the slender but strong chain of connections with various well-documented aspects of Shakespeare's life.

Short of decisive new documentary evidence, it is unlikely that the question will ever be settled. But that at least allows for a *fantasia* (borrowing Thornton Wilder's term for his historical novel, *The Ides of March*) on the events of these years – particularly on what a Campion and a Shakespeare might have had to say to each other: the intelligence of the martyr and the intelligence of the poet. And that is what this play attempts, without wanting to press the historical case too insistently.

Practically all the names are taken from Hoghton's will or other documents from the same period and area. Hoghton's exiled older brother was actually called Thomas, like the younger half-brother who inherited his estate; since this half-brother appears here, I have renamed the older brother William to avoid confusion. Similarly, I have rechristened Roger, Margaret Crichlow's husband, as Walter to distinguish him from Roger Livesey. There is a codicil to Hoghton's will revoking, without explanation, the legacy to Margaret. "Hastings" was one of several assumed names used by Campion in his travels.

It is worth remembering that this is a period in which accent has nothing to do with class. Lancashire gentry and servants sound much the same, and they will all sound rather different from a Midlander like Will or an internationally mobile intellectual like Hastings/Campion.

Characters

The Family

ALEXANDER HOGHTON, of Hoghton Tower
THOMAS HOGHTON, his younger brother
MARGARET (MEG) CRICHLOW, his daughter

The Household

ROGER LIVESEY, steward of Hoghton Tower
ROB TOMLINSON
MARGERY GERRARD
FULK GILLOM
WILL SHAKESHAFTE
THOMASIN
ALICE
SUSANNA

The Visitor

EDWARD HASTINGS / EDMUND CAMPION

The setting is Hoghton Tower, Lancashire: for these purposes, a general "Great Hall" space, door towards back, with hearth downstage right, settle, long table (downstage left), benches, a couple of stools; and a staircase to an upper level.

The action takes place between the winter of 1580 and the summer of 1581.

Scene I

[*Heavy knocks on a door. THOMAS HOGHTON – brisk, late fifties – enters noisily, discarding riding cloak, etc. To servants:*]

THOMAS [*loudly*]: Alex! Alex! Roger! Alex! Roger, where are you?

[*ROGER LIVESEY – in his forties; undemonstrative but capable of some very strong emotions – enters in nightgown, dishevelled and irritable.*]

ROGER: Christ's sake, Master Tom! D'you know what hour it is?

THOMAS: I'm not here for my health. Where's Alex?

ROGER: I don't care what you do or don't do for your health, but you might think about your brother's.

THOMAS [*slightly chastened*]: Aye, I know, I know. How does he go on?

ROGER: Not good. Six nights out of seven he won't be asleep till around now.

THOMAS [*pause*]: How long?

ROGER: Surgeon says nine months, maybe twelve, no more.

[*ALEXANDER HOGHTON – early sixties, heavy and formidable, slowed down by physical pain – has appeared at the head of the stairs, in nightgown.*]

ALEX: Nine if I'm lucky, twelve if I'm not. What the hell's all this, Tom?

ROGER: Master Tom can come up to your chamber; you need to be back in bed.

ALEX: Well I'm awake. What's the use? [*Comes slowly and painfully downstairs.*] Roger, get me a... [*looks around; ROGER pulls up a stool to the table*]. Ay, that'll do. Now, find yourself some work; the whole bloody house'll be awake by now thanks to Tom here. [*ROGER goes; to TOM.*] This had better be important or I'll have your guts.

THOMAS [*pauses*]: Have you slept?

ALEX: Not above an hour. Now: if I've got nine months left, I don't fancy wasting them waiting for you to tell me what you've got for me. Bad news, yes?

THOMAS: Tom Cottam.

ALEX: They've taken him?

THOMAS: Last week in Dover, soon as he'd landed. I guess he'll be put to the question any day.

ALEX: Christ. How do you know?

THOMAS: Letter from Jack in the Midlands. He sent it to one of our people in Preston and they brought it to me last night. I rode straight here.

ALEX [*pauses*]: You'll be needing something. Roger! [*Back to THOMAS.*] What's Jack Cottam after apart from prayers?

because by God he'll need those almost as much as Tom will. [*ROGER comes in.*] Get us some ale.

ROGER: Trouble?

ALEX: Bad trouble. Tom Cottam, Tarnacre.

ROGER: Aye. Taken, is he?

ALEX: Taken. It's his brother writing to us, the schoolmaster down in where is it, Warwickshire? [*To THOMAS.*] So what does he want? [*To ROGER.*] Ale.

THOMAS: Perhaps Roger should stay a moment. It's – well, it'll have...it might have something to do with the household [*Sits.*].

ALEX: How do you mean?

THOMAS: Tom Cottam came back to England with some of the, you know, the, er, the Company, and he sent one or two of them to the Midlands with his list of known men. Jack Cottam introduced a few of his lads from the school to them. So they'll have their names any minute once Tom's put to the question, if they haven't got them already. Jack says he'll stay there as long as he can, but he thinks the lads need to get out before someone starts taking an interest. Specially as he thinks one or two might be headed overseas. He needs an answer soon as we can.

ALEX: You're telling me he wants us to take them here? Bloody maniac. Doesn't he know they're watching us already? [*Turns towards fire*] As if, well, as if he didn't know about William, God rest his stupid soul. [*Back to others; more loudly.*] And so: we take on a few young men with accents from the midlands and suspicious backgrounds asking about passage on a ship to Antwerp or some such? God help us; Jack's as big a fool as William was. We might as well write to the justices and say, here's a nest of foreign papists, come and

9

collect them and while you're at it we'll be glad to oblige you on the rack and kindly pull out our fingernails.

THOMAS: Ay, well. Can't quarrel with that. But what he says is there's just one he wants us to take that he thinks might pass up here. Sixteen or so. Plays and sings, writes a good hand, he says, not just one of the yokels. His father's an alderman or something like.

ALEX: One of ours?

THOMAS: Well, Jack's got a bit to say about that. Sounds like the old man's playing both sides. He's paid the fines, but he paid for pulling down the images and whitewashing the church and all. Jack says he's a close old bastard and pays the fines for not going to church so that no-one has a chance to arrest him for his debts when he's out and about; says it's cheaper that way.

ALEX [*laughs shortly*]: Sounds like a proper hero of the faith. Is his son the same, then?

THOMAS: Jack says he's been listening to the priests when they come and he doesn't know what he should do, and he's...not happy with his father's ways.

ALEX [*sighs*]: Let's see this letter, then. [*THOMAS passes it over, ALEXANDER scans it, THOMAS wanders over to the hearth.*] Well; I see what he means about him passing up here; the name's nearly right. There's Shakeshaftes ten miles away. Maybe they've got a long-lost cousin down south that they're just about to discover. Roger, what do you reckon? Can we find room for a – what, for God' sake? Player, tutor, dogsbody? Along with that other lad from Chester who's coming?

ROGER: Happen we could. But you're not seriously telling me you want him here, are you? Him and his little trail of agents running after? It's no time for you to be giving yourself more to trouble you.

THOMAS: No, look, if we get straight back to Jack, today, we may be ahead of any agents. And by the time they've picked it up, he should be here and we can, you know, sort out the story. [ALEX *gets up, begins walking back to the stairs.*] But you'd better finish the letter.

ALEX: God, you mean there's more? What?

THOMAS: It's one of Tom Cottam's friends from the Company. He's travelling up here. He'll need a place to come and go from a bit.

ALEX: Jesus and Mary. So it's more of "Here we are, lads, come and arrest us," eh? [*Sits again.*] Come and pick up the servants and the family and find out what the old man's been saying in his cups, and.... [*Trails away, rubbing forehead, very tired.*]

ROGER [*fiercely*]: Tell them to go to hell. You've earned some peace; what business is it of yours if some fancy priest from overseas wants to come and stir things up? We can wait for changes. We don't need....

ALEX: Shut up, Roger [*Silence; reads; sighs*]. Thing is, I'll be dead in the year if they're right. There's not a lot they can do to scare me. And I'm going to have to face my Maker and say to him, I couldn't be bothered when it would cost me nothing or next to nothing. I don't fancy that. I've got enough on my slate to need a few good works in the balance.

THOMAS [*pause; then*]: Shall I get a message to Jack?

ALEX: All right. Yes. Yes, get him a message, today. We'll take his young man. And I guess we've no choice but to take this priest from the Company and all. Roger, you're sitting there like a wet Sunday. [*ROGER opens his mouth to snap back, thinks better of it, shakes head/tuts.*] Get some bloody *ale* for Christ's sake! And another gown. I'm cold. [*Rises slowly and starts for the stairs.*]

[*Blackout.*]

Scene II

[*MARGARET CRICHLOW – mid-twenties, can seem older, self-possessed, chilly – comes in, rapidly, followed by ROGER with ROB TOMLINSON, local tenant farmer, about ROGER'S age, awkwardly in the background.*]

MARGARET: You're telling me he won't see me?

ROGER: I am. I'll not have him worried at like a fox with the dogs.

MARGARET: *I need to see him*, Roger. He owes me that, for Christ's sake. Walter has to know about the money.

ROGER: Walter can bloody wait. You know how sick your father is, he's not slept again, he's got – he's got guests coming, I've business with Rob here to settle before noon, there's two new servant lads to see and I'm damned if I'm letting you upset the whole bloody household. Again.

MARGARET [*level and arctic*]: I'm not forgetting this, Roger. And I'm not just going away.

ROGER: Right now that's *just* what you're doing, mistress. There's no-one here with time for you.

MARGARET: Never is, is there? Never has been. But there will be soon. Think on.

[*She walks out: fast, bristling.*]

ROGER: Oh Christ Almighty. [*Sits heavily on the edge of the table; ROB walks closer.*] He'll have to see her some day, force of bloody nature, that woman. [*Gathers himself, turns fully to ROB.*] Anyroad, business. It's two weeks. He comes in two weeks' time. Edward Hastings.

ROB: Is that his name?

ROGER: It's his name while he's here. You know how it is.

ROB: So he's one of this – Company, then?

ROGER: That's what Master Alex says. I think they've told him who it really is, 'cause he's jumpy about it. If you want my guess, he's a big fish and there's a small army of government fishermen after him. [*Dry.*] Great news for the rest of us.

ROB [*flops down on bench*]: Can't get used to all this, Roger. You get these priests coming from France, Low Countries, wherever, dressed up like players, feathers in their hats and garters round their bloody knees, calling theirselves by all kinds of fancy names and laughing to theirselves. Like bloody players. And they tell us that if we go to the Sacrament down in the parish, we're – what did that last bugger say? – eating at the table of demons? [*Gets up, moves downstage.*] Christ almighty; poor old Sir Philip down the parish, he's a cloth-headed old sod as spends more time in the alehouse than the church, but he's no demon. Tell you what, Roger; you know I'm all for the old religion, else I wouldn't be here, God help me, but I can't thole these hard young men in fancy hats with fancy language, I can't see we need all this. All right [*looks round, lowers voice a bit*]; Elizabeth Tudor's a heretic perhaps, same as Sir Philip, and the service in English sounds bloody daft to me, but God looks after his own and likely when the Queen weds or comes to her senses, we'll –

ROGER [*interrupts*]: Look, I've said it all to Alex, Rob, more times than I've had hot dinners. But I don't know who's in the right. Fancy young gents from overseas, from the Company or the, what d'you call it, seminary, you can say what you like but they're not fools or cowards. It's not the hats and the stockings they think about when the hangman's cutting their balls off and sizing them up for quartering.

ROB: Come on, Rodge. All very well for them, if they want to risk having their balls off and their bowels out, good luck to them and no, they're no cowards. [*Sits again, looks at hearth.*] But it's us too. When the agents come, it's us they look at and it's our balls and bowels they may be sizing up and all. Like I said – like players: only, *they* know the play; they've read the story, and we've not.

ROGER: Ay well. [*Slips off table.*] Talking of players, the new lads arrived yesterday and I need to see them. Margery's bringing them over. Fulk Gillom up from Chester, and this young lad from down south, from Jack Cottam's school.

ROB: You said he was –

ROGER: Ay, he's got a name while he's here too, Will Shakeshafte. Should be easy to remember.

ROB: Is he some kin to Francis Shakeshafte over to Warrington?

ROGER: He might be. If it helps.

ROB: Like that, then?

ROGER: Like that and don't you forget it. You watch what you say about him or Hastings. Specially in the Charnock direction.

ROB: Crichlows don't know about this, do they? 'Cause if they....

ROGER: Better safe – here they come, anyroad. Bugger off, Rob, there's a good lad. And remember when Hastings comes – he's not likely to be anyone's fool, so don't play the fool with him. I'll collect you when I've done with these two. It's Ashcrofts this morning, with the fish to pick up.

[*ROB grunts, gets up and moves away to exit, as MARGERY GERRARD – twentyish, handsome, friendly but sharp manner – comes in with FULK and WILL; late teens, both of them, Fulk a bit earnest and slow, Will physically slight and restless.*]

MARGERY: Morning, Mr Roger; morning, Rob. These are the new lads just come. This one's Fulk, this one's Will. [*Grins.*] Will's the foreigner.

ROGER: Left you alone so far, have they? [*To FULK and WILL.*] Well let's have a look at you. Off you go, love. [*MARGERY exits, ROGER sits on bench.*] You know where you've come to?

FULK: Me dad used to come here years back. He was the man who made the dresses for the players in Chester for the summer plays. He used to bring the stuff up here in winter sometimes, when they were playing at the Hall for Christmas. I come once when I was ten, me and me little brother, and I....

ROGER: All right, all right, I don't need your life story. You can sit if you want. [*They sit at the table.*] So you know about the Hoghtons?

FULK: Some, sir.

WILL: Nothing much, sir. Except what Master Cottam says.

ROGER: And what does Master Cottam say?

WILL: He says the Hoghtons have one of the great houses in Lancashire, that they hold to the old religion –

ROGER: Like you do.

WILL [*pauses*]: Like – I do.

ROGER: Come on, lad, you need to do better than that if you're to manage here. I know you're here because Jack Cottam thinks there's danger for his young men who've been talking with the priests from overseas, but this isn't a safe place like Flanders or the bloody emperor's court. If you're here, you take the same risks. You need to know it's worth it. So do we.

WILL [*expressionless*]: Yes sir. I hold to my father's faith.

ROGER: H'm. What I hear, that still leaves a fair bit open. [*Pause.*] I know it wasn't your choice to come.

WILL [*the same*]: No sir.

ROGER: Well.... Anyroad, there's more you need to know [*Moves back to sit on table as before*]. Master Alex is a sick man. It comes and goes, but the doctor knows there's a tumour and it'll likely kill him. So you keep out of his way and you don't make trouble in the village. Anything that draws attention here is trouble, right? The agents will be around here and there and they'll be glad to pay us a visit and maybe more. Fulk, you know about the master's brother, that built the Hall?

FULK: Er... Master William?

ROGER: Ay, Master William. [*To WILL.*] He went abroad so as not to pay the church-fines, and they confiscated his land, and Master Alex and his other brother, they worked to keep him overseas so that he wouldn't come back and be jailed or hanged, but he thought they were after his goods, and they quarrelled and then he died last year. Which is why Master Alex is head of the family now and living in this Hall. Point is, after all that, there's a good many folk have good reason to keep their eyes on Hoghtons and what goes on in their houses, so you give them no occasion, right?

FULK: Right.

WILL [*moving away a little, eyes to hearth*]: Master Cottam says you have some other visitors.

ROGER: Does he now? Well that's the other reason you keep quiet. There's plenty to do here with teaching the youngsters their music, and writing for the revels and whatnot. And in case you're thinking, there's women enough here so you don't have to be down in the village all the time.

WILL: Who is it we teach? Is it the master's children?

ROGER: He's got none. Well, he's got one daughter out of wedlock, twenty something now, married to a man over by Charnock used to be cook here. [*Looks towards exit.*] Poisonous bitch. You don't need to know except to keep out of her way. No, there's the children of the gentry on this estate and the next one or two, that get sent here for their nurture, nine of them last time I counted, Woottons, Savages, Pembertons.

WILL [*turning*]: And the other visitors? Do they come here to…teach as well?

ROGER: Don't be too sharp for your own good. Ay, they come, and they have things to say, and the less *you* have to say about them the better. There's one coming next week. Master Hastings. Belongs to the Company, if that means anything to you.

FULK: What Company's that?

WILL: We had them visit back home. Big secret. Priests from overseas, only they call themselves the Company of Jesus, the Society of Jesus, and they make this promise to –

ROGER: I *said*, don't be too sharp. What the Company means for you and me is that from next week there'll likely be more eyes on this house than usual. So *you* watch and keep quiet. And if you recognise this man who's coming, this Hastings, you don't say a word, right? Now look, you'll find it strange these first days, specially you, Will, and they'll be laughing at your voice and what not, but don't fret and keep busy. Margery'll show you where you eat today and where you get your liveries and the rest [*stands; they follow suit*]. God keep you. I've to ride down to Ashcroft's with Rob and find out what happened to the bloody saltfish that's due.

[*Exit. WILL and FULK sit down again.*]

WILL: You didn't tell me about your father.

FULK: You were too busy telling me about yours. Cunning old bastard, your dad, by the sound of it.

WILL: Yes. Yes. I don't know – what he thinks about all this. I think when Jack Cottam said I should go, he was glad, though. Glad to see the back of me for a spell.

FULK: Why? Worried about you getting some lass – [*WILL looks away*]. Oh. Right. Leave it at that, shall we?

WILL: Tell me about the plays in Chester.

FULK: Did you have plays back where you come from?

WILL: Only in Coventry. I never saw them, but my father did, and my aunt used to make dresses for them sometimes. It's a while since they've been played there, though. You know. Popish.

FULK: Aye, same in Chester. But me dad remembers how it was with the old Queen, when all the guildsmen went to Mass in the Abbey on Whitmonday around five in the morning, and the carts started up and the Rows sounded like a thunderstorm with it all, and you stood and walked till near sunset, and ate in the streets and you could see the ones you fancied twice or three times over. [*Stands and wanders towards front.*] And back home, the rooms were up to your armpits in cloth and leather, and me dad and mam would be up all hours stitching and embroidering for the guilds that asked them. Your auntie must have been the same, then, up all hours and the rest. Did she tell you? Were you ever with her?

WILL: Don't think she and my father got on. But he talked about her sometimes; talked about the plays a bit, too. Biggest day in the year, he'd say.

FULK: Aye, same as me dad says. There was three days off work with it all. They say now you have to call it the midsummer plays, on account of there being no Corpus Christi any longer, I don't understand any of that, but last time it was still – well, still mostly what it was, for a while longer anyroad, only no more plays about Our Lady on account of it being popish, like you say. Five years ago, it was; they tried to have the mayor put in jail because of it, but nothing happened. Folk wouldn't let them. [*Pause; back upstage.*] Know something else me dad used to say?

WILL [*a little amused*]: Tell me.

FULK [*pause*]: Funny thing, I never really thought on it till lately, but he used to say as how this was one day in the year when every soul in Chester had the same story to tell. I couldn't make much of that, 'cause all the guilds had different plays to show, but he said it was all one story, and this one day of the year it was everyone's story, everyone's business. I thought, was it just that everybody had jobs to do in the same thing, you know, but he said, no, it were more than that. You look up there at the plays on the carts, he said, and what you see is you, you and your neighbours. 'Cause Adam and

Eve, they're you, and Noah and Our Lady and Herod and Maudlin and all, it's you, it's you making a fool of yourself and you saying yes to God and you saying no to God and you trying to keep him away and, and [*embarrassed*] aye, well, something like that.

WILL: Like you've got them all inside you, inside your head and your guts.

FULK [*animated*]: Aye, that's it, like they're all inside and then, sudden like, you see them all out there. Like a mirror. And you never knew.

WILL: Will they do them again, the plays?

FULK [*shrugs, turns towards hearth*]: Tell the truth, I don't know. Like I said, there's enough want it put down for popery, even if there's many as'll fight to have it still. But what I say is, what's popish about Adam and Eve and Herod and all those? There they are in the Bible. [*Pause.*] There they are inside and all, if me dad were right. Bits of what you're like. With only God knowing how it all fits together.

WILL: Yes. There they are. Inside. [*Stands, walks to join FULK at hearth.*] So what happens if there's no play? What happens to all those folk inside?

FULK: What d'you mean?

WILL: Christ, Fulk. A man would burst open if he couldn't see what he was like, if he couldn't get his insides shown him before God or whatever. If he couldn't see all that on the pageant, played out in front of him in this...mirror, like you said, and he could say, Yes, that's *me*, someone's seen me, someone's known what it's like, I exist. I'm here, not just in my head, but here for God and man and.... He'd burst open like – like a man on the scaffold, like a man with his insides being, being.... [*Shivers.*]

FULK [*startled*]: Steady, Will. It's only plays we're talking of.

WILL: Course. It's only plays.

[*Blackout*]

Scene III

[*MARGERY, THOMASIN, ALICE, SUSANNA – all late teens or early twenties – in foreground, other servants in background, talking.*]

THOMASIN: Which one, then?

MARGERY: Give over. They've not been here a week, hardly.

THOMASIN: Come on, Marge; you've seen more of them than we have.

ALICE: How much more is what I'd like to know. [*Laughter.*]

MARGERY: God you're dull, you lot. Only one thing to talk about.

THOMASIN: And the young lad from down south isn't dull? More things to talk about? Or is it more things than talking?

SUSANNA: If you ask me, he doesn't fancy ladies. I reckon he's got his eye on Fulk.

MARGERY: Don't be filthy, you stupid slut.

SUSANNA: Oh! You know better, do you?

MARGERY: He's all right.

THOMASIN: No more than that?

MARGERY: Like I said, it's less than a week, for Christ's sake! Anyroad, he'll come and go.... [*Laughter.*]. Oh God, shut up, you can't say anything with you, can you?

SUSANNA: So what do you know about this one that's arrived now? Must be something special that we've all been told to come and greet him like this.

MARGERY: I heard Roger say there was something special. That he's a priest with the Company, whatever that is, and the agents will be after him 'cause he's been around in the south and stirred it up.

SUSANNA: Stirred it up? Do you mean he's for the King of Spain or something?

MARGERY: I don't know, do I? I can't think Master Alex would have him here if he was a proper, well, traitor.

THOMASIN: Agents don't know the difference, though, do they? That's the point. I tell you straight, I don't fancy this. I don't want to be in front of the justices answering questions about whether I've been at Mass and being told I'm a traitor to the Queen if I have.

SUSANNA: Will we all have to go, then? To Mass? And confess and all?

ALICE: He won't have time to confess you. He's only here three weeks. [*Laughter.*]

SUSANNA: Straight, though? Do we have to go? Does the whole house go? What do I tell Sir Philip at the parish?

MARGERY: You tell Sir Philip nothing, right? Like as usual. Not that the old pillock'll notice any different, even if he's sober for a change. You tell nobody outside this house anything, no names, no times, no places. You act dumb. Shouldn't be difficult. [*SUSANNA swings at her and there is a short scuffle.*] Oh God, behave yourself, look it's Master Alex. And that must be him. Christ, he knows how to dress for a priest!

[*ALEX has emerged at the top of the stairs, HASTINGS with him, a middle-aged man dressed in the height of fashion. ROGER emerges from the knot of servants and bangs his staff for silence.*]

ALEX: Right then. Good day and God keep you. You're here to listen to Mr Hastings, who's our guest these next few weeks. But before he talks: you don't speak of him if you're asked down in the village except to folk you know for sure are our people. If Sir Philip asks anything, Mr Hastings is my cousin returned from the Low Countries, and he's a trader in jewels. The rest he'll tell you.

HASTINGS [*very formal and stately*]: Masters, brothers and sisters, thank you: you are generous to a stranger, and a stranger who may bring bad things to this house. You all know it as well as I know it, and I shan't make sport with you by pretending it's otherwise. Yet it is indeed jewels that I trade in. I am a priest of the Holy Roman Church and a brother of the Society of Jesus. [*Murmurs in audience.*] If I hide this from the world, I don't hide it from you, because for you, as the Lord says, I open my treasury and bring forth from it things new and things old, and to you I offer a pearl of great price. Why then do I hide it from the world? For fear of the pains it may bring me? Those pains are terrible to contemplate and I do fear them; I pray each day to be spared – not from the pains but from any fear that would make me false.

No: I hide this because your neighbours who do not share the gift of faith with you and me, if they knew me for who I am would sink further into error and sin by hating what they saw and seeking to do harm. For your neighbours believe men such as me to be traitors to our sovereign and our land. They believe us to be idolaters and liars, and so, as the Lord says in his gospel, they think that by killing us they do a good deed. Shall I drive them into this folly and blasphemy? No. I hide who I am for love of them, until such day may come as they can truly know what I am and welcome it. [*Walks down a few steps, spreads hands.*] So you, you must share this love and share this secret. For from you I hide nothing. I dress like a worldly man, and perhaps you will hear me speak like a worldly man, but you will know that this is only a kind of playing. You know that I am here for one thing alone and that is to make and keep you reconciled to Holy Church and steadfast in your religion until God opens the eyes of our neighbours and our governors.

So may God keep you all faithful. Tomorrow morning at five and every morning when I am here I shall offer the Holy Sacrifice in the upper parlour and I urge you all to be present. If you need to make your duties tomorrow and to receive the Body of the Lord, I shall be in my chamber tonight after six, ready to hear your confessions. Remember: if my life depends on your silence, your salvation depends on my liberty to speak while I am here. God save you and God save our sovereign Lady the Queen.

[*He and ALEX withdraw, to a buzz of comment.*]

ROGER: Now then: back to your work. Off with you; back to work straight and you may have less to tell Mr Hastings in your confessions. [*Laughter as they drift off.*]

SUSANNA: So am I safe then if I go to Mass? Nobody tells, right?

MARGERY: Nobody tells. Nobody tells anyone outside the household except that we have a jewel merchant here who's kin to Master Alex. And outside the household means Mistress Crichlow and all. She'll go to the Sheriff soon as wink.

THOMASIN [*half-laugh*]: God you're scaring me.

SUSANNA: Nobody tells, they won't know. [*Will and Fulk fall in with them.*]

WILL: They know already. The agents know where all the priests are.

THOMASIN: What do you mean? Do you mean we're all going to be taken and put to the question? I'm off if that's it, I'm off.

WILL: Calm down. They know but they don't need to do anything. They like you to know that they know, that's all, to keep you scared. But they won't take you or anyone unless it's time to let them in London know they haven't gone to sleep. And the further we are from London, the slower they get.

SUSANNA: How do *you* know, anyroad?

WILL: I saw a bit back home. They bide their time till there's talk of treason in London, then they look for a few locals to catch and serve up to the Sheriffs. And maybe then they have a good quartering to look forward to, and everyone can feel safe.

MARGERY: Good Christ! Are you trying to cheer us up or what?

WILL [*shrugs*]: It's how it is. Safer here than down in the Midlands because the justices here don't fancy killing their kin, from all I hear. And no-one fancies killing servants, so you can settle yourself. They don't need your evidence to hang a man.

FULK: Don't let him frighten you. We all go to Mass with closed eyes so we've seen no-one there, and we keep the rest inside. I don't say it's easy, but it's all we can do; and if some silly fool goes and leaves the household suddenly, that's one thing as'll draw the agents and the Sheriffs here in no time, so we stay and keep our counsel.

WILL: Right enough. Shut up the doors and light the torches. There's hard winter nights out there. [*The women leave, with one or two backward looks.*]

FULK: Will, you soft bugger. Do you want to keep them up all night panicking each other into convulsions?

WILL: They know what it's like. And if they don't, they need to find out. When the priests come, everything changes, all the words mean something different, no-one's name is their own. You learn your words and if you forget, you don't know what'll follow. They need to know that.

FULK: Come on. There've been priests through here times enough before, if what folks say is right.

WILL: Of course.

FULK: You're not convinced.

WILL: I'm not convinced. [*Pause.*] Old Roger thought I might know him. I do. Not just any priest, Mr Hastings. I met him down south; he had another name then. And Jack Cottam said he was one that the Queen herself would give a fortune to get taken.

FULK: God. Do you reckon they know, Master Alex and all them?

WILL: They will soon enough. Christmas games, Fulk, Christmas games. We'd better start learning our songs.

[*They go off. Blackout.*]

Scene IV

[*WILL alone, with wine-cup, on a heap of playing cloths; sound of singing and loud conversation off stage. MARGERY comes in, a bit drunk, sits down near him; silence for a moment.*]

MARGERY: Come on, they want you. They want another song.

WILL: Let them want.

MARGERY: Don't be like that. They love hearing you sing. We all love hearing you. We all love you, Will, some of us more than others [*small giggle*]. Are you going to be kind to us? Are you going to be kind to me [*hand on his arm*]? It'll be Lent tomorrow; you can make the most of it tonight.

WILL: Kind? Is that what it is?

MARGERY: Tired of your rough northern company indoors, are you?

WILL: No. No, it's... [*pause*].

MARGERY: What?

WILL: I can't hear. When there's a crowd like that, I can't hear.

MARGERY: You can't hear what? You've got two ears like the rest of us, haven't you?

WILL: I can't hear what they're saying. I can hear the noises, but I can't...hear inside my head. I can't hear where the noises come from. I can't...God. I can't....

MARGERY: For God's sake, Will [pause]. All right. Shall I go?

WILL: Do what you like. Go back to where people are *kind*.

MARGERY: I like being here. I like being with you. I want to listen to you. Even when you're as mad as you are now [pause]. Some of them think you fancy me. [Pause; awkwardly] I didn't know. Mind you, some of them think you fancy Fulk and all. I don't...I don't know how I can tell –

WILL: God. [suddenly flaring] God! It's a game with you, isn't it? It's a stupid bloody game with all of you. You think – Christ, I don't know – you think it's about *fancying*, like you fancy a meat pie or a new coat? Something you put on you. Something you put inside you. You don't know anything. Anything. I've heard women say it: I want you inside me, they say. And I want... [thinks; change of tone] yes, I want to be inside, yes, I do, I want to be in there, hearing where it all comes from, where it all.... And sometimes, whether it's a man or a....

MARGERY: Do you fancy Fulk?

WILL: For God's sake! No! Is that what they're saying? [Desperately.] How do I know? Do I want him inside me, do you mean? Me inside him? Yes, I want to know how I get to listen to where he comes from. I think of him for hours, how I can hear who he is. God, I think of you for hours, too. You, all of you... [fast, confused]. That's what happens, you know, when people meet. They want to be inside each

30

other but they're frightened to have someone else inside them because you know what it's like? Do you know what it's like for a man when someone wants to be inside him and you're stabbed through like a trophy, like something you bring back from the day's hunting? I've been.... Ah God, I can't....

MARGERY [*backing away a bit; not knowing what to say*]: Stop it, Will. I don't know anything about that. Don't talk past me. It's me here; not Fulk, not whatever man you...and not any woman from down south. It's *me* that can't hear.... I don't know what to make of you when you go on like this. I can't think.... But you know what it is to...to want to come into a woman...to...?

WILL [*savagely*]: I want to be in you. I want to be where I can hear you from way up inside your gut. I want to hear where you speak from [*pause*]. Perhaps I want that with Fulk too. Like you said when you were joking with your *friends.* [*quieter*] I don't know. All I know is I can't hear when you're all there, all making your game, your barley-breaks and your...your.... I want to be away from the noise. I want to be away from the wanting too. I don't want to go carrying bodies away from the hunting, jabbed through with a spear like, like hares or moles or, or....

MARGERY: Oh for God's sake, Will. Can't you be quiet now and just... [*touches him again, nervously*].

WILL [*pulls away*]: What? Be quiet and what? Do you think I can just quietly slip into you and say sugared things and slip out again and no wounds left, no traces on the skin....

MARGERY: Is it Father – Mr Hastings?

WILL: Is what Hastings? Do I want to be inside him?

MARGERY: My God, Will! You're as filthy as the girls. I mean – you spent all that time with him when he was here before, you used to hang on the edge of all that talk I can't understand. You used to listen to him as if your life depended. Is that what you want, to go off with him, to go overseas and be a priest and, and – then there's no more of all this, and....

WILL: And get the executioner inside me, inside my own guts and groping for my heart? That would fit, wouldn't it? The end of a man who wanted to be inside other people. Poetic whatever. No. It isn't Hastings. He listens, though. He can hear in a crowd. He's not interested in being kind either, not to anyone. I think he listened to me. I think he listened to something I can't hear inside me. But I don't know if that means I have to speak what he wants to hear. He doesn't know what I'm saying now. He doesn't know what it is to want like this.

MARGERY [*quietly*]: Whatever you want, Will; whatever you want. If you tell me to go, I'll go.

WILL: Don't go [*pause*]. I don't know where you are now, but I don't want you anywhere else. Don't go.

[*She puts out her hand. He begins to pull at her dress, uncertainly at first, then hard; kisses her savagely. She wriggles away. They face each other for a moment, then she stands and backs towards exit, beginning to unlace her dress. Blackout. The music outside fades and is replaced by something different, liturgical –* Tallis, In jejunio et fletu, *for example, or a Byrd* Kyrie.

The light comes up on the upper stage, showing HASTINGS, in Mass vestments, with the ceremonial bowl of ashes for the liturgy of Ash Wednesday: a handful of figures approach; to each one he says the formula, "Remember you are dust and to dust you will return."

WILL enters, carrying his shirt, downstage left. HASTINGS turns, meets his eye; locks eyes, pauses. WILL turns away and exits; HASTINGS continues. Lights fade.]

Scene V

[Evening, late spring. ALEX with WILL; papers on the table.]

ALEX: Good. It'll be as good a Whitsun as we can manage in these times. Two interludes?

WILL: Two. Mr Hastings thought we should have the second. I think it's something he wrote.

ALEX: Aye. [*Flat.*] He says he used to write plays for the Emperor's court when he was overseas. Not that I said that, Will, you don't know who he is, do you? And you don't know where he's been since he was here last.

WILL: Of course. I don't know who he is.

ALEX: Long way from the Emperor to Lancashire, eh? [*Looks sceptically at papers.*] I'm not too sure he's measured the miles if this is anything to judge by. Still and all. I'll not deny him the pleasure. He's here to keep us up to the mark [*pause*]. Has he talked to you?

WILL: Once or twice. Not for long.

ALEX: I think he's got his eyes on you. You know what I mean and what I don't. There's a good few have gone overseas for religion, Will, my own brother among them and your Jack Cottam's brother and all, and I can't make my mind up about it. Can't see much to hope for here in England, even if I wasn't coming to the end of my time. What I can see, Elizabeth Tudor's set for a long haul, and if she's not wed soon, chances are she'll never wed, whatever they say. And if she doesn't wed, there's nothing as'll make her change her mind on religion. If I was her, I don't know as I would myself, what with all these silly buggers running round with the King of Spain and the Queen of Scots and God knows who. So I can see why a young man who wanted to practice his religion properly might travel, even set up with one of these seminaries or with the Society. What I can't make out is why they come back and put us all in the way of the gallows and the knife. Shouldn't say this, I dare say. I know the man's here for our good, and it's a comfort to have the sacrament and all. But it strains a man's heart to be always looking over his shoulder and watching his words and – wearing masks. Christmas guising all year round, but damn-all pastime in it.

WILL: Perhaps...perhaps there's nowhere now... [*stands, moves away*].

ALEX: Eh?

WILL: ...nowhere to be simple. Nowhere where you don't have to watch your words and wear your masks. [*Abstractedly, gradually forgetting ALEX.*] Watch your words. You watch them like birds clustering and forming up for winter, or coming in to land or sitting so still on the trees you'd think they were wood or leaves, and all the time they're breathing, quick, soft, ready to spring up and fly, and you can't net them or bring them down with fowling-pieces and you can't get them where you want them....

ALEX: Will. What the hell are you talking about?

WILL: Sorry, Master Alex. Only it seems everywhere you go you have to make choices now that people didn't use to have. You can – see words out there, all the different ways you could talk, all the different ways you could make sense of the world, nothing fixed, and you in the middle of it, whirling

34

round and trying to catch a glimpse of something, something that's really there, only all the little dances and masquings of people talking to each other are hiding it and – and you have to feel the stream running under it all, like, I don't know....

ALEX [*deadpan*]: Much more of this and I'll be sending you overseas myself to get a bit of peace around here instead of listening to you rabbiting on like that. Anyroad, don't you go yet awhile, Will, all right? I can't see you in a black frock in the Low Countries, and I don't fancy seeing you in red trimmings on the butcher's block either. [*Glances at papers.*] Well, we'll have to live with that second interlude; dare say we'll cope. What about the music for the first one? We have the two viols, but where we get five extra singers I don't... [*door opens, ROGER enters, flustered*].

ROGER: Sorry, master. Mistress Crichlow, and she won't be gainsaid.

ALEX: God. All I need. Well, let her come. [*ROGER leaves.*] Will, we'll see each other in the morning about the rest of it.

WILL: Master [*bows and begins to move. MEG CRICHLOW pushes past him as she comes in*]. Mistress.

MEG [*to ALEX*]: Who's this?

ALEX: Will Shakeshafte. You've seen him here before. He's with us from down south for a spell to help with the playing and the music.

MEG: You mean he's another papist vagabond you're looking after and risking all our lives and goods. Perhaps you should remember that your property's not yours for much longer and if you put it at jeopardy we'll all suffer.

ALEX: Thank you, Meg. Do you know, I'd nigh-on forgotten I was dying. Will, off you go.

MEG: Wait for me below.

ALEX: Since when do you give orders to my people?

MEG: Since you started showing you're not fit for the governance of your own goods. [*To WILL.*] Go [*he leaves*].

ALEX: You know how to make yourself welcome, Meg. What do you want?

MEG: I need to know what you've done for us.

ALEX: What I'm leaving you, you mean?

MEG: Yes [*sits*]. We've a chance of buying Moss Side mill at Charnock. We need to know whether it's going to be a quarter of the property we'll have or more. We need to know this week.

ALEX: Christ, Meg. Can't you wait a few months? This is hard, even for you.

MEG: Even for me? Do you want me to pretend I've come to pay a kind visit to my ailing old dad so that we can remember the happy days of childhood?

ALEX: Come on, Meg. Your mother had a house and a good marriage to Beesley. It's not that you were left in a ditch with her.

MEG: I might as well have been. And you never knew what life in Beesley's house was like. Thank God for Walter. He's a fool but he leaves me alone.

ALEX: Don't start on that again. I can't say anything about what Beesley did or didn't. I didn't know then and I don't know now.

MEG: You've always known what you chose to know. Anyroad, I'll not waste time in that. What can you tell me?

36

ALEX [*angry*]: Why should I tell you anything? You want my goods, you might try and make a friend of me.

MEG: A friend? God help us. Too late for that. And I'm not likely to make a friend of a known papist in these times.

ALEX: You're still deep in with those bloody Puritan fools or whatever they call themselves now in Preston? Shaking the tree to see what more fruit you can get to fall. As if there wasn't enough already, lying on the grass and stinking because of you and your like, talking about reforming religion all over again.

MEG: Why should you tell me? What would you say if I said I was going to the Sheriff to talk about your guests?

ALEX: I'd say you always were a bitch but I didn't reckon you were a traitor.

MEG: Traitor? You have the gall to talk about traitors when there's enough traitors in your attics to hang the whole household.

ALEX [*rising, very controlled; takes her wrists*]: If you talk like that again, I don't care what you say to the Sheriff. Fleetwood's not a complete fool and he knows malice when he sees it and he's enough left of the old loyalties to his friends not to leap on his horse to Lancaster or wherever and fetch the agents. You try that, Mistress, and you'll not get even a quarter. You'll get my curse and a pennorth of rope to hang yourself if one of my people doesn't get to you first.

MEG [*equally cold, shaking off his hands*]: I need to know. You'll not threaten me out of my rights.

ALEX: You'll know soon enough. Now you need to leave. I'm a sick man, Meg, not just to spite you but because I am, and I need to go to my rest. Roger! [*ROGER opens door.*]

ROGER: Master.

ALEX: Mistress Crichlow is leaving. I'm for my bed [*walks upstairs heavily and silently*].

MEG: I told that lad to wait. I need to speak with him.

ROGER: You'll speak with him outside this house, not here. This isn't yours yet, and God grant it never will be.

[*MEG strikes him across the cheek. He stands still for a moment, then takes her by the arm, very hard. She winces.*]

ROGER [*face close up to hers*]: Not yet, *Mistress*.

[*He pushes her away and walks off. She stumbles, recovers herself, crosses the stage from the foot of the stairs. Light comes up on Will, seated, waiting.*]

MEG: [*breathing hard*] Come with me. Now.

[*MEG and WILL exit together.*]

Scene VI

[*MARGERY comes in, followed by FULK.*]

MARGERY [*flatly, arms tightly clasped*]: No.

FULK: I don't know, Marge, I only hear what they're saying. He's not – well, he's not just pretending with you, I know that. He's not one of those lads that, you know, talks himself into bed and then buggers off. And she....

MARGERY: No. He's been in her bed all right, I don't need anyone to tell me that. And you know why? Because he thought, "What'll it be like to be in her bed? I've got to know, I've got to know what it's like to be a betrayer, to know I've got another woman and I'm shafting someone else." I suppose it's the same with whatever poor cow he's got back in the south, I never asked about her. And you know something else? I think he asked himself, "What'll it be like to be in bed with a bitch who's going to betray me and all? What's it like to play with a woman who could give us all into the Sheriff's hands if she wanted? Who hates her father and everything to do with him?" He wanted to live in another world for a bit, that's what. He wanted to live in a world where there's no promises and no kindness and no, no... [*she chokes on her words for a moment; silence*].

FULK: I'm sorry.

MARGERY: Much use to me.

FULK: No, but I am.

MARGERY [*sits*]: You don't see it, do you? You think he's like you, you poor innocent sod. Or like me. You stand there, I stand here, and what I see, I see. But him, he wants to stand there *and* stand here and look out of your eyes and mine and – hers. Only you can't do that, can you? You can't step out of your skin? He hates living in his skin, I know that. In bed. It's like I can hear him rolling around inside his skin as if he were tossing round under the sheets when they get too hot. He says less and less to me, you know. Only when it comes to it, he bites and pushes more and more, God help me. Christ, Fulk, I feel I've been eaten alive. And now –

FULK: He was never going to stay, was he? I mean, you must have known he wasn't going to stay?

MARGERY: I don't know. I thought there was something I could do [*laughs harshly*]. God, that sounds pathetic. How many women do you suppose hear themselves saying *that*? I thought... [*pauses*]. I thought I might stop him going off overseas and risking his bloody life with Hastings and them. [*Turns her back to FULK; muffled.*] I thought it was God I had to worry about. Not Mistress bloody Crichlow.

FULK [*walks to hearth, leaning on settle*]: Well, say he has been...been with her. You know her. She doesn't *want* him. Not, you know, *him*. She wants to know what it's like and all, I reckon, what it's like to take what you see, take it in your father's face and...your God's. She's a walking itch, that woman, never rested, greedy for whatever's there because she's always been thrown the scraps. You get poisoned with scraps, I reckon, sooner or later.

MARGERY [*looks at him with surprise, a half-smile*]: My God, Fulk. Some things you do notice, then.

FULK: Ay well.... But if she has been with him, she'll not stay at it. What worries me is what she's going to get from him if she's minded. If she really wants to make life hell for her dad and everyone here.

MARGERY: Like I said. Where she lives, there's no promises. She'd see Alex out of here on the moors in his nightgown tomorrow if she could. Christ. I think she'd see him on the scaffold without a blush. [*Stands, brushes herself down.*] Do you reckon he's heard? Alex?

FULK: Couldn't say. I'd be surprised if he hadn't, but you can't tell, specially not now he doesn't move out much. It still looks to me as if he trusted Will. I guess he'll be – bleeding a bit if he does know.

MARGERY: Shouldn't he trust him? Do you really think she's pressing Will for something? Something important?

FULK [*pause, moves downstage*]: I can't say much. Only Will does know something about Hastings. He saw him down south, he said once, only he had another name then. So maybe if she got wind.... And if he didn't rightly know how much he was telling her or if he didn't see how set she was against her father....

MARGERY [*sharp*]: He's not a fool. And whatever I said, he's not going to send anyone to the scaffold if he can help it. I think – God, I think he'd feel the hangman's hands on his own body so much he couldn't do it, never mind anything else.

FULK [*turns back to her*]: Do you think she knows about Hastings and the meeting tonight?

MARGERY: I reckon. We're all bidden. He probably told her himself and all. Tell the truth. Strip the clothes off, strip the skin off. She won't come, though, and my guess is she'd be none the wiser if she did. You've heard Hastings. Talks like a man walking a rope: all obedience to the Queen's grace, no sedition, no word of judgment, nothing for the King of Spain to rub his hands over. All about returning to the truth that makes you free, so that nobody has to walk round in masks and disguises any more or come to Mass in the shadows with your cloak round you and your face hidden. [*Pause.*] All very simple. Only it's not.

FULK: Do you not think the old days will come again, then? Mass in the parish and Sir Philip's woman out of the parsonage and back with her sister, and the plays in Chester town and the monks back in the Abbey?

MARGERY: Tell you something, Fulk, things don't come back. Haven't you seen that? Hastings lets folk think it's about the old days coming again, all the good things, the times when we were just ourselves. Only it was never like that. It never was simple. Perhaps we never were ourselves. Christ, I sound like Will now. But what Hastings will bring isn't the same, and there's new – choices and new, I don't know, new clothes to wear and new things to think. Once you know it *could* be different, it's all changed. [*Pause.*] Like when you know your man's been in another bed. Things don't come back.

FULK: I'm sorry.

MARGERY: You said that. [*Moves towards exit; pause.*] We go in an hour, is that right? Ashcroft's?

FULK: Ashcroft's. There's folk coming up from Preston. Be a long night. Alex is coming and all, Roger's getting him ready, God help him.

MARGERY [*pause*]: I...used to joke about it, but I need to say. The girls and all. They used to...we used to say he fancied you too.

FULK: Ay. I had heard.

MARGERY: And?

FULK: And nothing. [*Rallies.*] Tell you something, though. You don't have to be in bed to think you're being eaten alive. You can eat a man by listening, did you know that? You can eat a man through his eyes. And you can not know yourself, not know who you are by the time it's done. [*Silence.*]

MARGERY: I'm sorry.

FULK: Much use to me. As they say. I'm going for my boots. [*Pause.*] He wasn't ever going to stay.

MARGERY: No.

[*They go off separately.*]

Scene VII

[*ALEX, HASTINGS enter with ROGER and others, WILL hanging back. Cloaks, gloves, etc. removed. ALEX and HASTINGS sit on settle by hearth, ROGER pours wine, exits. WILL sits on floor. First few exchanges as others drift off.*]

ALEX: Well. Well. Do you think the Queen's Grace will thank you for that?

HASTINGS: The Queen's Grace may thank me or not as she pleases. I spoke my thoughts.

ALEX: Did you?

HASTINGS: I spoke my thoughts and they all listened hard. Look. You know and I know that she has no passions in matters of religion. I've met people who stand close to her, people who see her in her closet. She's shrewd, she's careful of her safety; she knows when the ground moves under her, she has to move with it or be swallowed up. Christ, I know there are fools enough who talk about war and invasion and calling on the King of Spain to sort it out, God help us; and there are – well, I can hardly call them fools, can I? – in Rome who talk very large about these things as well, as if some idiot's knife or bullet would put an end to.... But fools is what they are. And I'm not, Alex, whatever else I am, nor is Elizabeth Tudor. If the ground moves...and it will, if enough of these folk believe they can find their way back to the old religion without blood and treason.

44

ALEX: Good argument, maybe. But since when has she or anyone ruled by argument? She rules by....

HASTINGS: She rules by show and ceremony and high state, like every prince since the beginning of the world. I know: I've seen it, you've seen it. Princes are magicians, specially in these days when you can buy the sparkling toys and the machines to make people gasp. I saw it in Prague with the Emperor, poor softheaded soul. But –

ALEX: But there you have it. You don't get a magician breaking his staff by choice. You don't get a player stepping away from the centre of the stage when he's in full spate. You've seen it, you've seen her. She loves that stage. They all love her on it.

HASTINGS: But think of it. What if your players here came out in front of you with no lines learned? Never seen the parts they were to play? What if they'd never even seen a playbook? I tell you, this realm tore up the playbooks fifty years back and no amount of pageant and state and jewelled dresses and fine allegories and magical machines will make up for it. Come on: she knows that half the courts in Europe call her bastard or whore or both. She knows there's one thing she can't buy and flaunt like another jewel, and that's legitimacy, Alex, legitimacy. There's no lawful ground beneath her, no playbook to say she's speaking her part right. So she goes on spinning her webs for all she's worth, a spider furiously stitching up all the little broken twigs, with more and more little bodies hanging on the web. It's like what she wears, all the pearls hanging by little threads, all the lace so thin you could tear it with a fingernail. If you were she – if you were she, don't you think you might be ready, sooner or later, to trade all that, all the terror and the panic of an actor on stage with no part learned, no part written, would you not think of trading that for recognition? For the courts and the Pope to look on and say at last, yes, I know what she's saying, yes, this is a true performance, she knows her lines?

ALEX: Ay well, like I say: she won't thank you for that. She'd not relish being called a spider, and I dare say she loves her clothes and all. But you see, I'm not so sure about her, Edward: I think of her and I think, you can love all this even when it's panic and fear; you can be excited all the way up your virgin insides, if that's what they are. And whose recognition is it that matters? When all the courts in Europe have had their say, it's these folk here in this realm who look at her and see what they know and what they want. These are the ones she worries about at night, not some foreign papist holding his nose.

HASTINGS: But if they, the ones she worries about, if they start to see that there's more that they want, there's more than she can give them maybe, if they see that she....

WILL [*awkward and louder than he meant*]: Father. Can I... what....

ALEX [*startled*]: Eh? God, Will, I thought you'd gone.

WILL: No, I – listened, when you were talking back there, and then I....

ALEX: What, then? Make sense to you?

WILL: Oh it made sense. But only if – if you know, if you really know, so that you'd die for it, only if you know there really *is* a playbook. But what if there isn't? What if you really are pushed on that stage and no-one could have told you your lines anyway because, because there wasn't....

ALEX: For Christ's sake, Will! You're not turning Lutheran?

WILL: I'm not turning anything, sir. I want to know how you know the playbook's there, in Rome or wherever. Perhaps it's only what someone else did, what someone else said, hundreds of years ago, when they were on their own on a stage and there were no playbooks. And – you know spiders? They spin it out of themselves, don't they; they get it out of their bowels and....

HASTINGS: What's in those bowels, though? You know your catechism. What's in any of us except lies and tales and images of who we are, that we set up and worship? God, these reformers are simple! As if idolatry were only bowing down to images and paintings, not bowing down to what you see in the mirror, what you find lodged at the back of your imagination. What comes out of that nothing that's in the heart?

WILL: You want me to say "nothing," I know. But I don't...I don't think it's like that. Perhaps you see just that: that you're nothing and there's only despair inside and so you have to – well, to look around and find someone else's eyes and find an earth and a heaven and....

HASTINGS: A new heaven and a new earth out of your own bowels, eh? That's a clever spider, Will, but I've not met any spiders except the ones that spin in the dark corners for a night or two and then get swept away. All right: speaking of a playbook may be a foolishness, because I know about plays and you and your friends do too, but I'm here to tell you, and all those folk there tonight, that there's something they can trust that isn't just their bowels and isn't even just their prince. [*Pause: then, deliberately and unconvincingly light*] And if I didn't think that, d'you reckon I'd be risking my own bowels for it? Eh?

WILL [*silent*]: –

HASTINGS: All right. It's late. Alex, you're three quarters asleep.

ALEX: I'm four quarters confused, I'll tell you that.

HASTINGS: Will: come back when you're ready. I still have some things you need to hear, whether you think so tonight or not. Help Alex to his bed.

WILL: Yes. [*Pause.*] I don't make light of it, you know. I'm not mocking. The pains, I mean and what might....

HASTINGS [*turns away slightly*]: All right. All right. I know what you mean and what you don't. Come back when you can take it.

[*Blackout.*]

Scene VIII

[*MEG alone. WILL comes in, looks around.*]

MEG: No, just me. If they told you Margery was looking for you, I expect there was a mistake.

WILL: What do you want? I can't tell you more. You know I can't.

MEG: There's more to tell, then.

WILL: You can twist my words as much as you like. I'm not pretending. There's no more.

MEG: You know about twisting words, I dare say. This house is full of people busy twisting words. You could make a bloody bedcover out of all the plaiting and knitting-up and fancywork here. They say that, you know, about papists. You can't tell if they're atheists or double agents or treble because they give all their skill to making these patterns of words that cover up the plain things, cover up all the treasons and devices. Who knows what they are when they're not playacting?

WILL: And you? Who knows what you are? So you've decided to play the rejected bastard, like the cheap stories they show in the innyard. The bastard plots for his inheritance and the husband gets cuckolded and the wife schemes for freedom and the servants get drunk. Don't tell yourself, don't tell me, you haven't decided who you're going to be. It's not a difficult part to play.

MEG: Alex said you talked nonsense. [*Pause.*] You know what was done to me.

WILL: I know what was done to you. Why does that make you who you are? You still have to choose what to do.

MEG: Oh yes. So I do. So do you. I choose to stop arguing philosophy with you and you need to choose – you supposedly clever man – whether you want me again and what price you're ready to pay.

WILL: I don't pay.

MEG: Very high-minded. You don't pay Margery, and you don't pay whatever whore you have back in the Midlands and you expect women are never going to ask you. But some of us will, you know, some of us who don't reckon ourselves so lucky to have you in bed that we don't think of payment. Come on, Will. [*He is silent.*] I tell you what, I'll help you put your hand in your pocket for me. You said you'd seen him before?

WILL: Who?

MEG: Hastings. You said you'd seen him.

WILL: I never told you that.

MEG: There's others can talk too. Don't lie. You'd seen him before. So. You're not what anyone would call a travelled man, so you saw him back in whatever sorry shit-heap you lived on in the Midlands. So what connects that with here, that's the only question I've got left, because if I can answer that I'll have some information worth having. The only question is whether we both get something else along the way that might be worth remembering. [*Moves towards him.*]

WILL [*flinching*]: I've no more for you. I don't want any more...remembrances. [*Shakes off hand on his arm.*] I don't want you [*more and more harshly*]. I don't want you, I'm not going to betray anyone to keep your bloody inheritance safe. And if you think your father will give you what he's promised if you go to the Sheriff or the agents, you don't know him. He's not afraid of dying, but I tell you something else, if it comes to breaking faith with his God and his honour, he won't mind the rest of us dying either.

MEG: He broke faith with his wife. That's why I'm here. I don't know whether he'll give me what I want, but I do know his faith's a little bit more fragile than you say. It's worth trying.

WILL: He's your father. Wait; keep your thoughts to yourself, he'll do his duty by you. Try and force him and you'll have blood on your hands and nothing else in them.

MEG: Do you know, I thought a shopkeeper's son might be easier to manage than a gentleman. You're as stupid as the rest of them when it comes to it, aren't you?

WILL: He took me in when it was asked. He honoured his friendships. He's been good to me and to Fulk....

MEG: And to Mr – Hastings. So he was honouring friendships when he took you in. Thank you. So who does he count for a friend in the Midlands? [*Pause.*] Cottam; Jack Cottam of Tarnacre, went for a schoolmaster in – where was it? You're one of Cottam's boys, that's it. You won't tell me but it's no great matter to find it out. I knew you'd tell me something, Will, and I'm grateful. But not that grateful. That doesn't count as payment. [*Caresses him in passing; WILL stares at her.*] So what shall I do with this little windfall? Once the Sheriff hears, he'll have to act, whatever Alex says. He'll find out who the big men were among the papists who've been through the Midlands these last few months and he can do well out of it if they net one of the great fish. I dare say you've heard of Mr. Campion? Edmund Campion? No? [*WILL motionless.*] Quite a story. They talk about it even in Preston, do my friends. He was at the Emperor's court, they say, and now he's here, been in England a year or more, leaving his little pamphlets on the seats in churches and begging for a disputation with the scholars in Oxford. Mr. Hastings writes, doesn't he? Perhaps I might be persuaded, do you think, if I could see what he's been writing.

WILL: You know nothing. Hastings is Hastings, that's all I know.

MEG: Oh Will, you can do better than that. As you said: no one is who they are. No one's name is their real name. I am not what I am, yes? What I want to know is who was it who decided to be Hastings and come here to bring deceit and sedition. And when I know that – well, I may find out a few other things about my father and his household. And my future. You know, you were right earlier and I was wrong. You don't know what was done to me. But you were right too. I choose who to be. And I do not choose to be a slave in my father's house or my foster-father's – or my heavenly Father's for that matter, if you understand anything about such things. [*Pause.*] A pity you wouldn't pay. I thought it a fair bargain.

[*Exit, leaving WILL alone in silence for a long moment.*]

Scene IX

[Late at night. HASTINGS in settle by the fire, in shadow, with wine, alone. Behind him the door opens and WILL slips in.]

HASTINGS: It's no good, Will. [*WILL starts.*] You'll never make a servant in a great house. They know how to walk without noise.

WILL: God, Father, you gave me a shock. What are you doing awake at this hour?

HASTINGS: Come and drink some wine. What am I doing? I'd guess something different from what you've been doing at this hour. Meg or Margery? [*Pushes bottle and cup towards WILL.*]

WILL: What?

HASTINGS: Meg or Margery? Or is there another I've missed? I hope it was Margery if I'm allowed any preference.

WILL: Meg is...Father, Meg wants to know who you are so that she can use it to force her father –

HASTINGS: Yes, it's all about her inheritance, no? Not a stupid woman, even if she's a murderous one. How much did you tell her?

WILL: What do you mean?

HASTINGS: Well, some women have a way of finding things out in bed. So they tell me. I wouldn't know, of course. My guess is you told her more than you expected to. They tell me that happens in bed too. But it's no matter, I'm moving on the day after tomorrow. Back south. [*More quietly.*] Things I need to finish there.

WILL: What about the papers you....

HASTINGS: I'll send for them or come back for them. You've looked at them?

WILL: Yes.

HASTINGS: Any clearer about where you'll be?

WILL [*longish pause*]: I can't come with you.

HASTINGS: Tell me.

WILL: I can't. It's – it's not Margery or....

HASTINGS: I didn't think so.

WILL: Doesn't all that matter to you?

HASTINGS [*gets up impatiently, paces*]: For God's sake Will! I'm not a first year novice in a nunnery. Men do what they do; if there's enough in them, they find out sooner or later how to keep out of bed with boys or women, once they know where they have to be. Don't you think I've seen worse than you and your friends, ten times over? You long for the game, then you need to come and confess it, then you'll do without it when you have to. And you – I know something of men like you, men who know that when they get out of bed, whether it's a boy or a woman, they feel they've spent something of their soul and the day comes when they don't want to waste it any longer. Is that right?

WILL [*low*]: You know it is. But I said it isn't that. If I knew, if I knew that all this, what the Company does, bringing this country back to the old religion, if I knew that was the, the story, the one story that would bring it all together, yes, I'd be there, I'd be away from women and the rest, I could make sense of [*pauses*] –

HASTINGS: What they'll do to me some day soon. You don't have to be tactful, Will; I think of it quite often, you know.

WILL: Yes. But wherever I look, it seems there isn't one story. The old religion is the only, the only – picture of things that speaks to me, yes, but it's as if there were still voices all around me wanting to make themselves heard and they don't all speak one language or tell one tale, and all that – it would haunt me if I tried what you do, and it would make me turn away from the pains and the question, because I'd know that there'd always be more than the old religion could say and it still had to be heard... [*trails away*].

HASTINGS: You remember a couple of weeks back, we talked about spiders. Spinning worlds out of their bowels. It's a good picture, Will, but it's not what gives you hope. [*Sits again.*] You may hear all these other voices. Do you think I don't? But it's not every voice that tells how things really are. "Test the spirits," says Scripture. Oh yes, I can quote Scripture when I have to as well as any Lutheran or Disciplinarian and a damn sight better than poor old Sir Philip. Test the spirits: test the voices. Some will let themselves be drawn in to harmony and some won't; and the ones that won't you have to leave alone. God speaks harmony. It's one thing we do know, you and I, yes?

WILL: Yes.

HASTINGS: Music talks to us, yes? It tells us how it all should be, as if it's God's hint to us of what he purposes, and when we talk and write, we think music is where we should be and music is what we should sound like. And there's a cost to that. Not every voice comes in. I preach sermons about the saved and the lost, we all do. And when you get past the noise of parsons shouting, what's that about? Some voices are going to be out of tune for ever. Leave them, don't seek them out. They'll soften your heart in all the wrong ways and you'll forget that there's a truth at all.

WILL: But what if they're – shut out of the harmony because no-one's let them be heard? What if the only way to...this harmony you talk about is like letting God bring it about when every human spirit has its voice. So what *you* thought was harmony turns out to be less than what God can do? And for that to happen, you've got to listen to the ones that are – like you said – "out of tune"?

HASTINGS: So you get to stand in for God meanwhile, is that it, conjuring spirits out of the deep in great armies so that the harmony is bigger and deeper than Mother Church can guess? You get to put us all straight and show us how small our world is? Brave thought. Good luck with it. I shan't call it arrogant, because I don't think that's what you are, Will. But God gave his Church firm guidance, he gave us fathers and teachers, the creeds and the Pope and all of us priests, however stupid and sinful we are, because human hearts aren't made just to keep the door on the latch for all the voices there might be out there, however mad they are. [*WILL starts to speak.*] No, shut up, Will, I want to hear what I'm going to say, because I'm not sure I know myself where I'm going. [*Pauses; a half-smile.*] The air's full of noises, full of spirits, and some send you mad, so you can't tell what's real from what's not. Truth, Will; that's what we're fighting about. I hate the Lutherans and the Calvinists and your half-witted Puritans in this ramshackle church here, but there's one thing I don't hate about them and that's that they know they're fighting for truth. They're wrong about it, but they know it matters; and they don't shrink from the pains of the gallows and the block either.

WILL: So theirs are the voices you shut out?

HASTINGS: We have to. The devil has his choirs as well, and they can make you think for a moment that there's harmony there, or that there might be, but it's a song of the sirens. It's shipwreck that way.

WILL: But...once you choose which voices you listen to, once you decide what clothes to wear, what beliefs to put on in the morning, how can you say that one of them is truth?

HASTINGS [face to the fire, quite quietly]: You don't *choose* like that. You [glances at Will, then back to fire] – what do I say to you? – you surrender to the harmony you hear, you don't make it up, you don't write it like a tale or a fable out of your – [smiles] well, out of your bowels, as you elegantly put it.

WILL: And what if you just can't help hearing more all the time? If what's asking you to surrender is just...well, bigger than what you and the others say, bigger than the harmony *you* can imagine? It's not that I want to make up the world out of my bowels. That was a foolish way of talking. I know I have to listen and when I listen I have to surrender. But, but I don't know what it is that I submit to, not as if I was surrendering to you or the Pope – or the Archbishop or John Calvin or some mad clerk at Cambridge.

HASTINGS [pauses, quite long]: All right. So this isn't the time when it's clear. All right, Will, I don't want you with me if you can't hear this, if you can't catch the harmonies. Because you're right, you're going to be asking every moment, have I heard right, have I heard enough, and that's not the state of mind that holds you upright on the scaffold. But what is there here for you? This nation's a sad place, people seizing what they can and shouting loudly about their freedom, and a ruler who paints her face and looks around for a mirror, not knowing from one day's end to the next what the world is except her theatre, where she has to keep you all entertained, because when she stops entertaining you she'll die and so will you. Do you think this realm can last with that kind of rule? Do you seriously reckon you or anyone can hold up the other kind of mirror to her now that'd show her the truth?

WILL [*slowly*]: What if you could? What if you could make her say, This is me?

HASTINGS: Don't hold your breath. How would anyone do that, now it's all gone, the feasts and the saints and the Mass itself? Because those are the real mirrors, that's where you look to see who you are. Look, you've heard what I hope for and what I don't, and I mean it. I hope she can be spoken to, that something will get through that great web she's woven and let the light in. But I know – well, I know at this time of night, anyway – the chances are pretty small. I know you can't just bring it all back in a night, the feasts and the abbeys and the pilgrims. I know whatever comes will be different. Perhaps after all the killings it'll be – I don't know, quieter or something. Because there'll be plenty more deaths – mine, probably, and your schoolmaster's brother and a few more, and the Society will go on sending us and the Queen will go on killing us. [*Pause; he gets up to walk downstage.*] Here, in this nation, if you're not with us you're against us – more Scripture for you. But if you're not in with the ones who want the old religion, who is there, what is there? An endless servile dance around an ageing courtesan. The old ways falling apart and poor men abandoned on the roads and the people's wealth streaming into the hands of the Queen's favourites, and buying ships and guns for stupid, stupid wars....

WILL: I can't tell, Father. And the guns and the wealth and the courts – are you telling me the Catholic princes are any better? You ought to know. What with the Emperor and all. It's not as if this is the only sad nation in Christendom. What if we're all doomed to be sad now, sad and stupid? What if there's no way back to the old ways, if they ever were what we say they are? And the only thing now is to try and find room for the sadness to be – to be *there*, to be in front of your eyes and in your ears, so, so you know you're, I don't know, not asleep.

HASTINGS: So you go back to the Midlands, you get some lass with child, you marry and take over the business, and you look and listen for all this when you have time to spare from the children and the merchandise and filling up your barns with grain to sell off dear when there's a bad harvest? There are plenty of things to make you deaf after a while.

WILL: Perhaps. Perhaps on my deathbed I'll think, you know, he was right, that Father – Hastings. I'll think, hell, I've got it all wrong. Or perhaps I'll have forgotten what to listen for by then.

HASTINGS [*looks at him hard*]: Not quite that, I think. I don't think you forget things. But remembering them won't come easy for you. So I don't know what you'll do with all this, Will. I don't know where you put it. I just pray you don't bury it. Ask yourself.

WILL [*pause*]: You leave the day after tomorrow?

HASTINGS: I do. If I don't see you tomorrow, Will, you have my blessing for all the God-knows-what that you're going to do and my prayers that somehow or other you won't forget whatever it is we've been saying, and at this hour of the night I don't know any more than you what *that* is. [*Pause; slight smile.*] And if the harmony ever starts up, you know where to find the brethren. Even if you won't find me. Give me a prayer when you can. I'll be needing it.

[*They stand. Silence. WILL quickly kisses HASTINGS'S hand. They go out by separate exits.*]

Scene X

[*ALEX in his bed, visibly weak; ROGER, THOMAS.*]

ALEX: Will he talk?

THOMAS: People do. I know he's a brave man, they mostly are, but once the experts have got to work, they'll get something, even if he doesn't know what he's told them.

ALEX: So how long do you reckon we've got?

THOMAS: Far as I know, they took him three or four days back. So it could be a week or two, depending who wants to talk to him. Did you know he was that big a fish? Been putting the universities in a fit as well as the court ever since he landed, by the sound of it.

ALEX: Ay, well; he told me a bit, did Edward – Edmund, I should rightly call him, I suppose. The Emperor's court and all that. Young Will knew something too, he'd come across him back home, he said once, when he was using another name. And he knew about the Emperor.

ROGER: Will knew something?

ALEX: That's right. Why?

ROGER [*awkward*]: I'm sorry. I've got to ask.

ALEX: Meg, right?

ROGER: Ay. Meg. I did wonder.

ALEX: You can go on wondering. I trusted him, and I think I was right. Don't trust his judgment, though, letting himself get caught by her. 'Cause I never trusted her, and I was right there and all. But God knows what she got from him and how. Like you say, Tom, folks don't know what they're telling sometimes when they start in with the instruments. And I reckon it's easier getting men out of the Tower in London than when they're snared by some woman who's going to have their guts out in the other way. God knows why men go for it. I'd have spared him that, but I couldn't find the....

THOMAS: It's true they had something on Edward from here. They knew who he was when they followed him down to Berkshire. And the only one who'd want to talk from round here is Meg.

ALEX: She's already called. Roger saw her this morning.

ROGER [to THOMAS]: Ay. She wanted to speak to Master Alex and I wouldn't have it, I told her where to go. If she's going round with her own version of the rack or the needles, I'm not having him troubled, not now. But she made it clear enough who we'd got to thank for the news.

ALEX: Roger wants me to die in peace, God bless him [ROGER pulls away angrily]. I dare say she wants me to die and all, whether in peace or not. And I'm with her there. There's nothing to do now for Edward – Edmund, I should say – or Tom Cottam except pray. There's the will, though.

THOMAS: Signed and settled?

ALEX: Signed and settled, four weeks back, after he went off south. In case. And the two lads go to you if you'll have them, to Heskeths if you won't. [THOMAS tries to interrupt]. No, don't say anything, you don't have to decide till things get clearer. Till I've gone, anyway. So long as it's there and you know it. Where they go from you or Hesketh and when, that's up to you.

THOMAS: What about Meg?

ALEX: That's what I wanted you both for. If I'd known all this for sure four weeks back – I guessed she would if she could, but I didn't know. Couldn't know till he was taken. She gets nothing, right? I want you as witnesses. Whatever's written down there, she gets nothing, and she'll have to go to law with you both sworn against her if she tries anything on. Problem?

THOMAS: No problem. But you could get the lawyer and straighten it all out on paper.

ALEX: No. [*With effort.*] Lawyer comes, sees what's there, and if I don't die in a week or two there's plenty of time for him to let her know. He's closer in there with that Puritan lot than he lets on. So she finds out, there's time to make mischief for me and all of you. And the lads and all. Do it this way, with you swearing to what I said, and anything she says is going to sound like malice. You can drop a hint or two to the Sheriff about her and Will, and they'll think I'm getting back at her and they'll not want a thrown-off mistress tying up the law for months. If I change it and she sees it, she sees the plans for Will and Fulk, and she'll have grounds for setting them on to the two of them. As things stand, the will's made before anyone gets arrested or hanged, nothing suspicious you can put your finger on in law. No, she can wait, so long as you two will swear. Let her think I was afraid to cross her, let her think she's going to get what she asked. And with good luck, the lads will have moved on by then.

ROGER: Will won't stay up here. Fulk'll go back to Chester, I reckon, but Will....

ALEX: Nothing doing with Margery, then.

ROGER [*laughs shortly*]: Christ, you don't miss much, do you? She'll get over it and nothing to show.

ALEX: Nothing to show, eh? All these months with Edward and Will and Fulk and the rest and nothing to show. No wounds on the body, is that it? Everything under the skin and life goes on. For some. Everything out of sight under the skin; or is it under the playing clothes? [*Pause.*] Well. Off you go. If I'm going to die in peace, Roger, I'd as lief not do it just this afternoon to oblige you. I need to sleep. [*They begin to leave.*] I'll see Will and Fulk in the morning. You can tell them. [*Pause.*] God help us. Bloody times.

  [*Blackout.*]

Scene XI

[*Much activity, servants folding bedlinen, etc. MARGERY enters, obviously distressed, shaking off ROGER's hand.*]

MARGERY: I told them, I bloody told them, I said, he's not twenty four hours dead, I said, how can you come in here and expect us to turn inside out for you, and they just, they just.... One of them said, "Well, he's in luck, then," and he said, "that's more than I can say for the rest of you."

ROGER: I know. It's how some of them do business, these agents. Like no-one's ever told them you need to behave like human beings when there's birth and death and stuff around. I know you did your best, love. Have they all gone?

MARGERY: Thank Christ, yes. I tell you, Roger, if they'd stayed much longer I'd have had the kitchen cleaver out, and so would the rest of them. [*Pause; breathes hard and collects herself.*] How much trouble is it, Rodge? Really?

ROGER: Alex did his best. I don't reckon they'll find any papers here, whatever Meg Crichlow's said. And they've not asked after – after the lads.

MARGERY [*pause*]: He's gone already. Of course. Do you know where?

ROGER: Tom took him, but he'll not stay there, I know that. Back down south, I should think.

MARGERY [*makes towards stairs*]: I need to turn out the chamber. Sir Philip's asking when we want him buried. He's been poking about and all. I didn't say, I thought Master Tom would settle that. Only I wondered about –

ROGER: Don't fret. There's a priest in Lancaster as knows and he'll do the necessary when he can.

MARGERY [*sits*]: They've all gone. The master and Father Edward and – and Fulk. And Will. They've all gone. What do we do, then?

ROGER: You knew he'd go back.

MARGERY: Ay, I knew. Is that supposed to help me?

ROGER: Come on, love. Like you said, they come and go. Don't get me wrong, but we've all had too much happening these last months, and now Master Alex is gone, God rest him, and old Hastings or whoever he really is – not that I'm glad he's in those bastards' hands in London, but you know what I mean....

MARGERY: I don't think so. I don't think so. You might not have noticed but things don't go backwards. Will used to say that, when Father Edward tried to tell us it would be all right once the Queen or someone like that had seen the light. You...you see something as was covered up before, and you think, it doesn't have to be this, I don't have to be this, I can dig inwards and find what I never met before and you can't stop seeing it. Or I can look at you, Roger Livesey, and think, God, what's in there, then, if you start digging? [*Half-laughing.*] What's going on behind that grey face, maybe it's all festivals and dances in there, only he never lets it out and perhaps he's laughing inside at the rest of us. And when I see him, I think, Christ, I don't know him, though I see him every day of my bloody life. And that makes everything, makes it, I don't know, more dangerous, more, more....

ROGER: What the hell are you on about?

MARGERY: Forget it, Rodge. Having you on, you silly old bugger. But still. What do we do, eh? When we know there's something behind the curtains. Behind the – eyes. Father Edward had an answer. You peel yourself down when you confess and then you dress up again only you dress up in what he tells you to wear and you turn into someone new who does all the right stuff and tells their beads and signs the pledges to pray and goes to Mass and keeps away from the parish church and has a list of saints to help you along for every day of the week. Always someone to tell you who you are in case you forget, shove your name in front of you with a list of your jobs. Only, like, like Will used to say: when you know you're choosing it, you know you don't *have* to choose it and it's another kind of play, another set of curtains and you're still nowhere nearer who you are.

ROGER: So he wasn't much use sorting it out either, was he?

MARGERY: Who said you could sort it? But you have to look at it. Inside, outside, you have to look at it. No one to tell you who you are, but you can look. That's what he thought. [*Pause.*] But you know something, Roger? You can drown that way, like you want to jump into a river if you look long enough from the bridge. Jump into the dark inside you and everyone else. Like he did with Margaret and me. And whatever else he did.

ROGER: Don't blame him for all this; it was bloody Meg, you know that.

MARGERY: Sometimes I imagine him talking to her, looking into the river of her, jumping in before he knew what he was doing. Betraying someone in his sleep. And is that when who you are comes through, then, when you're asleep? Sleepwalking? Oh God, I'm losing it. [*Stands, walks up and down a couple of times, hands against sides.*] Sorry Rodge. You don't deserve all this.

ROGER: Talk away, love. We're all at sea these days.

MARGERY: At sea. Ay, that's it. You can remember what it was like to stand on solid ground, only there isn't any to be had any longer; and you look over the side when the wind drops and see your face and a great empty sky behind it. [*Silence.*] I was going upstairs. Clean around a bit. Stop thinking who's not here, isn't that right?

ROGER [*with effort*]: All right. Say you...you look over the side, like you say. And you don't just see your face but...other folk's faces. All at sea, eh? All of us, you, me, Will, Edward. And the ship...goes on, like. And what you can trust is the wood and the nails and the sailcloth.

MARGERY: Christ, Roger! You can turn it when you've a mind to.

ROGER: No, I don't rightly know what I'm saying, love. But does either of them need to be right, Edward or Will? Or Mistress bloody Crichlow? Or the Queen or the agents or the King of Spain or.... The ship's going and one day it's going to run aground on the side of a little bank of earth six feet long, every bloody soul on board.

MARGERY: Ay, well. But folk won't stop looking over the side. And they'll think like Father Edmund, what's down there, what keeps it all moving, or they'll think like Will, is that really my face in the water or his or hers next to me and how do you know the difference. [*Pause; then half-laugh.*] So it doesn't get quiet on board.

ROGER: Not drowned yet, eh? It's a start, love. Keep at it, so you don't get drawn to jump overboard; keep singing so the sea doesn't get into your lungs, is that it? Do you reckon they'll keep singing? Edward and Will? When Edward's under the butcher's cleaver? Or Will's making gloves with his dad in the Midlands and saving money to pay for whatever poor baggage he's got pregnant and wondering what he could have been if he'd stayed here or gone overseas with the Company or whatever?

MARGERY: Singing doesn't come easy to anyone these days, far as I can tell. I reckon we need the nails and the cloth and what not. But it's worth listening out for. 'Cause when folk do sing in times like this, maybe it's worth stopping for.

ROGER: Bloody times; that's what Alex would say.

MARGERY: He wasn't wrong. Only when are they not? [*Pause.*] I've got to clear the chamber.

> [*She starts up the stairs, leaving ROGER seated. From above, she starts singing, "In youth, when I did love"; ROGER smiles wryly, sits and listens to the first verse, then joins in the second verse as he walks off stage and MARGERY begins to come down the stairs, arms loaded with bedlinen; the lights fade to blackout as she finishes the song, alone.*]

> In youth when I did love, did love,
> Methought it was very sweet,
> To contract, O, the time for my behove,
> Methought there was nothing more meet.

> But age with his stealing steps
> Hath clawed me in his clutch,
> And hath shipped me intil the land,
> As if I had never been such.

> A pickaxe and a spade, a spade,
> For and a shrouding sheet,
> O and a pit of clay for to be made
> For such a guest is meet.

THE FLAT ROOF OF THE WORLD

The Flat Roof of the World

NOTE

David Jones, born in London to a Welsh father and an English mother, studied at the Camberwell Art School and then served in the First World War. He was wounded in the catastrophic action at Mametz Wood in July 1916, in which the Welsh Division lost some 4,000 men. After the war, he went back to work as an artist and joined the Roman Catholic Church. In the 1920s he spent much time as a member of the small community of Catholic artists and craftsmen around Eric Gill, first in Sussex and later in the Welsh borders at Capel-y-ffin. He was engaged to Gill's second daughter, Petra, but she broke off the engagement in 1927.

The effect of this, combined with the ongoing traumatic impact of his war experience, was a lifelong anxiety and vulnerability, though he was supported by many loving friends. Valerie Wynne-Williams, a young Welsh actor and athlete, became close to him in the 1950s, but he remained an essentially solitary man, increasingly unable to leave the security of his rooms.

His works as a visual artist and a poet are utterly distinctive. His long poem on the First World War, *In Parenthesis*, published in 1937, is widely regarded as one of the most significant artistic records of the trenches.

How far, if at all, he was aware of the complex currents in the Gill family (Eric Gill sexually abused his two eldest daughters), no-one knows.

Characters

VALERIE: Early twenties; Welsh, exuberant, slightly at sea in some conversations.

DAVID: Thirtyish for some scenes, sixtyish for others; middle-class London, compulsively hesitant, a mixture of very articulate and very inarticulate.

PETRA: Sometimes nineteen, sometimes indeterminate middle-aged; self-possessed, statuesque, faintly ironic.

ERIC: Mid-forties; aggressive, confident, afraid of intimacies.

Scene I

[*David's room in Harrow: a couple of sofas loaded with books and papers, a cupboard, sink, a hard chair, a table covered with collapsing piles of paper, bookshelves.*

A doorbell rings. David comes in with Valerie; he is awkward, fussing ineffectually; she is amused, slightly impatient. She heads for a sofa.]

VALERIE: Oh, you shouldn't have!

DAVID: What?

VALERIE: Cleared a whole six inches for me to sit on.

DAVID: Sorry, it gets a bit...I mean, I like to have the books and stuff where I can, you know, um....

VALERIE: It's all right. Really. Joking. [*She moves a few papers. DAVID winces visibly, VALERIE grins at him, picks up a sheet of paper.*] Is this one of yours? [*He nods.*] Duwedd annwyl: looks like the sofa; piles of stuff all round the edges. There's a hell of a lot going on.

DAVID: There always is. That's why it's so bloody hard.

VALERIE: Hard?

DAVID: You look at something and then you see something else showing through or creeping in at the edge; you get one thing down and it shouts out for another. [*Takes the paper.*]

No reason ever to finish, really. It's supposed to be, well, um, it's the, you know, it's the Annunciation, Mary and the angel Gabriel, only you see, all round the edge? [*VALERIE looks, exclaims.*]

VALERIE: I didn't see them. All those *bloody* beautiful little birds, it's like....

DAVID: It's Mary somewhere in Wales, sitting on a hill, a hill like the one near where we used to live, when I, when we, er, when I sort of started really, well, painting, seriously painting, you know, properly; thinking properly, painting properly. It's Mary, waiting on the hill; it's a girl waiting, on a hill in Wales. [*Pause; then, speeding up.*] And look, Gabriel's dressed like a deacon at High Mass, ready to sing the gospel, because it's good news, you see, and then, look, can you see the – sorry, you're not, um, you're not a Catholic, are you, sorry, I ought to explain, it's, er....

VALERIE [*smiles*]: Take your time.

DAVID: Sorry. No, sorry, I er, I get a bit, um.... Michael not with you today?

VALERIE: No. No, I wanted – well, I wanted you to myself a bit. [*Turns away; beat.*] You know, I'm only just realising how bloody *famous* you are. [*Turns back.*] You might have said. I mention your name to people and they're so impressed, "You go and visit *David Jones?*" they say.

DAVID: And you thought I was just a pathetic old buffer who liked going on holiday to Wales. Yes, I should have said. "You realise I'm famous, so just shut up and bloody listen while I lecture."

VALERIE [*laughs*]: You know what I mean.

DAVID: I do. I'm glad you didn't know. Famous. Well, I don't know. [*Pause; awkwardly.*] You, um, going to marry him, then? Michael?

VALERIE: Not sure yet. Possibly. Probably. Not today, though. I thought I'd have a day off from the twentieth century. I want to listen to you rambling on again about Thomas Aquinas and King Arthur and plainsong and whatever. But we could start with a cup of tea.

DAVID: Well; yes, um, good idea. Let me just, um....

[*He excavates a saucepan from under the table, fills it at the washbasin, lights the gas ring with difficulty.*]

VALERIE: *What* the hell are you doing? Haven't you got a kettle, for God's sake?

DAVID: Well, I did have one, but it went a bit...I, it was, well it got a bit, um, so...I mean, it's difficult, I don't really, you know, get out as a, as a rule, and the shops are a bit, well, they're difficult these days, and....

VALERIE: David –

DAVID: Sorry. I mean, it does *boil*....

VALERIE: David, I am going out. Now. To buy you. A kettle.

DAVID: Oh: no, er, you really don't have to, it won't be very long....

VALERIE: It's not for me, it's for the next poor bloody girl you want to show a good time to. Don't go away.

[*Blows a kiss. She goes out. PETRA enters from upstage, stands behind DAVID. They do not look at each other.*]

PETRA: Well well. Lucky man. Is she going to be different, then?

DAVID: Different?

PETRA: You know. Not like me or Prudence or whoever else. She's quite a change from Prudence, though, God rest her, not quite the aristocratic porcelain. Sorry, not fair. But is she going to *grapple you to her* at last? I can remember a fair bit of grappling. But never coming on board. [*Smiles.*] So to speak.

DAVID [*embarrassed smile*]: Well, yes. Yes; I mean I don't know but I do remember. It's just, this isn't, I'm not exactly what you'd call a seaworthy vessel, am I? Mast's been down for quite a while now. Oh God, think what your father would have made of that one... [*breathy short laugh*]. But it means I just have to keep rowing; and when you row you have to look backwards all the time. Fog everywhere as well. So you can't tell what's ahead, when there's a voice or a noise, you can't tell if it's a boat that'll need room and you can't tell whether they'll hit you. You can't tell if there's some bloody great thing coming up in front of you that you can't see, and you, you... [*shivering*]. You have to wait. Sit in the sodding fog....

PETRA: Like at Mametz.

DAVID [*with difficulty*]: Mametz....

[*Change of lighting. D. in spot, standing, looking forward.*]

July 1916. Up before it's light, before the mist starts burning off. Orders to advance up the hill in slow formation, wide open to the German guns. No cover.

They promised a smokescreen but it never happened.

You can't hear anything. Sounds odd, bloody great explosions going off all the bloody time, all around, but there, inside the fog, in the dawn, walking forward as if you were on cushions, walking on air, walking on the flat roof of the world. And then – like being hit on the back of your legs, like the boom in a boat swinging loose and just catching you there, so much weight, and you don't know what's happened until you feel the liquid running down and pooling round your toes, oh, you think, Christ, I must have been shot, so that's what getting shot is like, like being knocked off a boat in the fog.... Then you have to crawl because you can't walk, and the rifle gets in the way and pushes your helmet up, and you have to drop it, it's the worst thing of all, it's like dropping a girl, leaving it when you promised you'd never.... That's what the instructor said, treat that gun like your wife, he said, cherish it till death us do.... [*Pause.*] The corporal who hauled me up, he didn't say much but I think he was from Carmarthenshire, lovely accent that, like Valerie's, and he stumbled along till we bumped into this major, and he said, "Corporal, what the hell do you think you're doing? Drop the bugger here, and he can bloody well wait for the stretcher-wallahs. Don't...."

[*Lights come up.*]

PETRA [*in unison with DAVID*]: "Don't you know there's a sod of a war on?"

DAVID: Ah. When did I first tell you that?

PETRA: Don't remember. Early and often, like voting in Dublin. Whose line was that?

DAVID: Don't remember. You know them all, don't you? I used to worry that you'd have heard all my stories before we got married, and then what would we do for the next fifty years?

PETRA: I used to think I knew a lot about you. I'm not sure what I know now. Things have happened. Look at me now:

I'm a fat middle-aged housewife. I think I'm pretty happy on the whole. I don't think about you every day. Is that terrible?

[*Beat. PETRA comes forward; spot on her.*]

Yes.

People sometimes say, people who think they know you, I never really understood why it didn't work, why you didn't.... You seemed so settled, you seemed like an old married couple.

There's an obvious answer, I suppose. Well, several obvious answers. I used to feel like one of those characters in fairy tales sometimes, enchanted and locked away, with only my loom, clattering away – making trousers for you, remember [*turns briefly to DAVID*], remember when I used to do all that weaving every day? And you said the trousers were so thick you said they could stand up on their own?

There was that girl in the story, remember? Who had to spin all the time, spin straw into gold? God, think about it, filthy, clinging straw from the floor, where the goats had been, and the hens and the rats. You knew about that, didn't you? Living on the straw and listening for whatever; literally. I know I'm just talking and you lived in it and bloody nearly died of it. Only that *is* what it felt like, I don't know how else to talk about it. And then someone comes to the door and – asks for you as if you really existed, and for a moment you think it might be different...and then nothing really changes, and things just drift on, only now there's this sort of itch because you know there could be a way....

Pa understood; of course. Well he thought he did, as usual. Never one for self-doubt. What's that thing you used to talk about, negative something or other...anyway he really didn't have that, did he?

[*Lights up. Sofas pushed back, one or two hard chairs. DAVID (younger, wrapped in heavy overcoat) at table, now a work*

80

bench, cluttered with tools, blocks for carving, stray sheets of paper, paints, paint brushes in jars. PETRA moves in and sits on a chair.]

PETRA: How is it?

DAVID: Do you know, I think it's coming: I didn't think I could do copper, this thing keeps slipping; it's so not like wood. But it's really coming, look, the lines are looser, and this kind of cross-hatch, that works, doesn't it? Don't know what your pa will think.

PETRA: You'll find out soon enough [*takes out cigarette case*]. Have you got a match?

DAVID: Ah, yes, er, somewhere... [*roots around on table, various things fall off*]. Oh Christ. Sorry, they're here.... No, they –

PETRA [*retrieves matches from under the table*]: Honestly, Dai. Were you really in the army? I'm amazed we won.

DAVID: That's pretty much what my sergeant-major used to say. "If the Huns win," he said to the platoon, "you'll know it's because Private Bloody Jones can't tie his effing bootlaces." He believed everything joined up, you see, that sergeant: bootlaces included. Real philosopher. Get anything out of true and the whole thing...well, you know. I got better; but I could never do parades; nightmare for everybody, dropping stuff and turning left when they all turned right, like Charlie Chaplin in that stupid film, remember? Perhaps if the war had gone on a bit longer, I'd have, well, I'd have –

PETRA: Died, probably. Anyway, I don't think Europe would have thanked you for keeping the war going until you could tie your –

[*Perfunctory knock, ERIC enters.*]

ERIC: I'm not interrupting anything, am I? Just wanted to see how the engravings were doing. [*Moves to table.*]

DAVID: No, let me just clear....

[*Too late. Eric has picked up a sheet of paper.*]

ERIC: Oh for Christ's sake, Dai! You're not still doing sodding *watercolours*?

DAVID: Well, yes; yes, I thought it would be a good, er....

ERIC: It's not a good anything, Dai. It's just bloody decoration. What do you think you're *making* when you paint one of these? It's just...wallpaper for some capitalist collector; it's not a thing with a purpose.

DAVID: Sense.

ERIC: What?

DAVID: Sense. That's what I'm making. Trying to see straight. Trying to find where it connects, where what I'm seeing fits together and, and...releasing something. Look, you lay it on really wet, like this, then it sort of leaks around, and then you can see, nothing's *just* what it is, nothing just sits there, it joins, it – bleeds, it, it....

ERIC: Christ's sake. Spare me the philosophy. You know what we're supposed to be about here, don't you, what this community is about? Not *art*, God help us. *Making*: making what works, what fits, what – you know what I mean. Making things that have a good clean *use* to them. Things where you know what they're *for*. Those engravings, I wish I could get you really working on stone or something again, but at least they tell a story, you can see the point. But *watercolours*....

DAVID: It's no good, you know, I can't do arguments, you know that. It's just what you can't help, when you look, when you look through a crack and you see....

[*Forward; spot on D.*]

Looking for firewood; you had to do a lot of that over there. There was a barn, not very big, and I thought someone's bound to have stacked something there, or there might be old cartwheels or something like that. It was in a bad way, I think it must have taken a couple of shells at some stage. Only there was a light inside, you could see it through the crack, and I sort of wondered what was going on, and I put my eye to it, and there was – there was a figure in a kind of fancy dress, one of the padres I'd sort of met once or twice; candles, a few people kneeling in the straw, you could hear a kind of mumbling, foreign-sounding stuff. There was a big old thug of an Irish soldier that I knew, boozy as hell, always in a fight....

It was something religious, I knew that. Just not religious like Sunday School in Brockley. Didn't have a clue. It's just that they were all *doing* something, all right, yes, *making* something. Only not a something to use for something else, just a something, a pattern where all the paths light up and the whole thing – breathes, or whatever. That's what I want to do, I thought, that's what I want to do, *that's* –

[*Lights come up.*]

ERIC: You know what, you're not *thinking*, that's your trouble. [*Pause.*] Talking of thinking, I don't suppose you two have thought about a date? You said you'd sort something out after you got back from your parents.

PETRA [*forestalling* DAVID]: Don't nag him, Pa. You know there's all sorts of things we have to – to get straight before we –

83

ERIC: For God's sake, Petra! You don't want to hang around for ever, do you?

PETRA [*sharp*]: You want me to get on with what I'm *for*, is that it?

ERIC [*uncomfortable*]: It's you I'm thinking of; both of you. And yes, why not? It *is* what you're for. No shame in that.

PETRA [*neutrally*]: No shame.

DAVID: Job to be done, yes? Grandchildren and the rest.

ERIC: Well, there's nothing wrong.... All right, that's not quite.... But – look, you both know you need to get a move on. You've got a duty, Dai. And yes, yes, what *are* women for? After all, you don't go to her to talk about ideas, do you?

[DAVID *starts to protest*]

PETRA: Yes, I know. I'm a lump. A handsome cow. Time for the bull [*looks at ERIC*]. Or I'll turn into what's her name, Penelope, weaving all day and unpicking all night. [*Looks at DAVID.*] Maybe that's what I should do, start unpicking the clothes I make for you. [*Dreamily.*] Pulling the threads out all night long; long threads, one by one.

ERIC: All right, that's enough, we're not getting anywhere. I'm only saying. We need to know. Petra, your mother wants you in the kitchen. See you at lunch, Dai. [*Awkward, fingers watercolours again.*] Nothing personal. I mean I know you're not trying to make things difficult. Only, well –

DAVID: Yes, yes, don't worry, I don't, um....Yes.

[*ERIC and PETRA downstage, light down on workshop area.*]

84

ERIC [*begins to roll a cigarette*]: I don't know what's got into you.

[*Beat. PETRA looks a bit longer than is comfortable; ERIC looks away.*]

PETRA: You know I heard from Denis?

ERIC: Made up his mind about leaving the monastery, then?

PETRA: M'hm. He wants to come. You know he asked –

ERIC [*overlapping*]: Yes. Your mother said.

PETRA: Mummy says I should take what's on offer. Before I'm on the shelf. At twenty: confirmed old maid.

ERIC: So you and David haven't –

PETRA [*overlapping*]: What do you think? No. No. I don't know what he wants. Nor does he. [*Pause.*] Nor do I. Denis seems to.

ERIC: I knew *he* wouldn't last as a monk. Picked up too much in the Artillery. Do you know, when he went to the monastery he left his hat with David, to be collected when he was thrown out, he said? I expect –

PETRA [*quiet, not passionate*]: Oh stop it, stop it, stop being so bloody knowing and smutty and, and....

ERIC [*hasn't got it*]: He'd be all right, you know, Denis. Do the necessary.

PETRA: Fill the place with grandchildren, you mean? After all, what else is there? The only way of – joining things up.

ERIC: Oh God, not you too. I've lost you.

PETRA [*flat*]: Yes.

[*Pause*]

ERIC: I mean, Dai's problem –

PETRA: Careful.

ERIC: Dai's problem is just that, really. You heard what he said, for Christ's sake, about things – leaking into each other. So you can't see what *this* is for and *that's* for, and you can't see anything without being, I don't know, haunted by all the other things, and you end up paralysed.

PETRA: Haunted? Are you surprised he's haunted? You know what he saw. You've heard him talking about –

ERIC: Often. [*Grins.*]

PETRA: No, don't, just don't. *You* never saw it, after all. It wasn't like being an RAF driver in Dorset [*ERIC bridles*]. All right, not fair, and I know Uncle Kenneth died in France and all the rest, but.... Bits of men hanging from trees. It's really not quite the same, is it? Treading in what's left of the man next to you. Waiting with a bullet in your leg, not knowing if they'll come for you or you'll drown in the mud or get a bayonet in your spine. *I'd* be bloody haunted. I'd be wondering if it all joined up anywhere. If the bits in the trees could be – put together. [*Voice breaks; silence.*]

ERIC [*hasn't been listening*]: It's like his workshop, really. Everything everywhere, blocks and chisels and brushes, bits of paper, books, matches, bloody *watercolours*, for Christ's sake. Nothing in one place.

PETRA: That's it, is it? Keeping everything in its place, no dangerous leaks.

ERIC [*puzzled*]: Well yes, or you – as I say, you don't know what anything is for, do you, you don't have the proper map, you don't –

86

PETRA: Keeping things separate. Yes. Yes. I can see that.

[*Looks at him steadily. He looks away, walks offstage. She follows slowly. Lights come up on DAVID.*]

DAVID: When you woke up after two hours, with a big push ahead of you and every likelihood of dying, it took a long time to shake off the night, shake off the sort of *thickness* inside and all around. It used to feel as if you could never do anything *exact* again, anything that needed you to concentrate; that it was going to be unbearable to do anything like cleaning a rifle or threading a needle or even finishing a sentence. When dawn arrived, it was as if only then could you start telling one thing from another and you knew that as soon as that happened you could all start killing each other again. That's why walking through the fog could feel like, I don't know, burrowing back into another world. Where nothing had edges or boundaries, and things were still possible, where you were walking high, high above the landscape of territories and passports and armies and battles and sharp metal to cut you in pieces and hang you on the trees. The roof of the world. Isn't that what they call the Himalayas? There we were, conquering Everest. Until the fog lifts and the light and the rain come, the rain all sharp like tiny little bullets, cutting the blanket open. And you'd look at the wood around and say, here it comes, like a knife down the joins, laying it all open, cutting it all apart. If only you could see and not cut it open. Or only cut it to set it free. We used to joke at Capel about freeing the waters, unblocking the streams around in winter and how it was like conversation suddenly set loose and running round in the light and....

[*Lights come up again. VALERIE returns, brandishing a small electric kettle.*]

VALERIE: There we are: one kettle. Ket–tle. Remember them? Like your mam used to have. You fill it with water, then you plug it in and it boils the water: like magic. Where's the socket?

DAVID [*flops down on the sofa*]: Will it boil the food of a coward?

VALERIE: What?

DAVID: *You* know. Taliesin, *The Spoils of Annwn*? The cauldron in the Underworld that Arthur goes looking for. "It would not boil the food of a coward." [*Talking rapidly, increasingly fluent.*] Supposed to be the origin of the Holy Grail thing, this bloody great pot in the Underworld, with nine virgins guarding it, and if you throw dead bodies into it they come back to – well, actually that's in the Branwen story really, though you remember Taliesin crops up in that too, long before you get the Arthur connection, and there's this thing by W.J.Gruffydd where he says – you remember? – about the other cauldron in Ireland that comes out of the lake with – oh, what's his name, and –

VALERIE: I love it when you talk about all this stuff, I really do. But I hate to tell you, not everyone in Wales has read Taliesin. Not even me.

DAVID: But you're a nationalist; you know why it all matters, you –

VALERIE: You mustn't believe all that some of your nationalist friends tell you. Down in Merthyr Tydfil, they really don't all speak French and go to Mass and read the *Mabinogion*. Most of them probably think things like that should be against the law.

DAVID [*agitated*]: But then, I mean, you're not serious, what's...I mean it isn't funny really, is it? And it isn't a day off –

VALERIE: Sorry – ?

DAVID: Day off from the twentieth century, that's what you said, wasn't it? Yes, I know you weren't being serious, I know, but, but what's the *point* of all this nationalist stuff if it's only the bloody *Daily Mail* in Welsh, or, I don't know, Welsh subtitles for second rate Hollywood films or, what's his name, Elvis, Elvis Presley, or Harold Macmillan? Just talking balls in Welsh?

VALERIE [*gently*]: I'm sorry, David. I didn't mean to make fun. Only – isn't that how things work? Languages stay alive because people want to talk balls in them, not just to – I mean, you understand that, you wrote about it all, all those blasphemies and jokes and music-hall songs in the trenches, all of them *saying* something, tying things together, echoing big things, just not always trying to *say* big things, just letting it show through.

[*Bends down to plug in kettle; pause.*]

DAVID: "It will not boil the food of a coward." The trouble is – Valerie. Darling lovely Valerie. *Cariad*. I'm so bloody scared of all *this*, all this that I live with, I mean, look at that picture you were looking at, I'm scared by it, do you understand, scared it won't – hold, won't sort of *set*, I mean it's, what it's about, what it shows, that's wonderful, but what do *I* do, caught in a thicket like Abraham's bloody ram, and I'm just scared all the time, you know? scared of everything out there and even more scared of everything in here [*touches head*], scared that there isn't a way of holding it all together, or that there's no way through to those people you were talking about who want to forget the *Mabinogion* or whatever, no way to connect with all those people living with machines and jobs and, and *Daily Mail*s and, and....

VALERIE [*sits on arm of sofa, touches his arm tentatively*]: David, I'm so sorry, you know I don't mean to upset you. I meant it, I want to listen to you, I want to.... [*turns aside for a moment; then moves to sit on DAVID's lap. They kiss slowly, then stretch out on the sofa, embracing. After a moment, DAVID struggles free and sits up, breathing hard.*]

DAVID [*trace of panic*]: *It's not boiling.* You see?

VALERIE: What? *Cariad.* I didn't switch it on. [*They sit for a moment.*] I'm sorry, I shouldn't have. Too much. Just that you looked so – desolate. [*Silence.*] Is it always like this? I mean –

DAVID: You see, though, don't you? I never know. Am I a coward who's just scared as hell of lying down with a woman? Or is the coward thing to, to leave all this and settle down and keep the good old world going? Do what the twentieth century expects. [*Pompous military voice.*] "The Twentieth Century Expects that Every Man will do his Duty." Fulfil your purpose, continuation of the race, whatever, doing Good Work [*sketches quote marks with his fingers*].

VALERIE: Was that what it was with – Petra?

DAVID [*eyes ahead, doesn't look at VALERIE*]: I couldn't think of *being married.* I couldn't imagine, literally. I thought about – well, about the obvious: I could imagine that all right [*laughs briefly*]. Most of the time. There aren't that many topics of conversation in the army, after all, I'd got used to *that.* I just couldn't – think about having, you know, different priorities, things that had to matter more than, well, *this* [*waves arm at room*]. You see, there's nothing for me to do, nothing for me to *be* for, except this, trying to hang on in the middle of all the breakage and the forgetfulness to something that holds it all.

I suppose that's what you learn in the army, what I learned in the army anyway: find the words and say them and things happen, things change. Or at least you know that you've found the word that really echoes, that really *carries* what matters. I used to think that was why there was that one word soldiers used all the time, you know, the one adjective that fits everything, the unprintable one, the F-word. The Efficacious Word. Joke. It really does work, for every situation, so why not use it to death? As it were. But what I really mean is the way in the trenches something was said and then it was so. The words do what they mean or mean what they do. Those are the words I'm looking for all the time, all the time. And the forms, the shapes, doing all this lettering – God, even those watercolours old Eric used to bollock me about – shapes that just show things slipping into each other, like fish into water, like beautifully carpentered wood sliding together in a join. Never got the hang of that with wood and so on. But what else is there to do? Eh? What else is there? I know people think yes, work and sex and children and sex and money and all the rest is what you do, but it's *not what I do*, it's not what I'm for....

[*Pulls himself together, half-turns*] Sorry. I get worked up. But that's what it was. What it is. Not just Rosy.

VALERIE: Who on earth is Rosy?

DAVID [*small laugh*]: Short for neurosis. It sounds a bit more friendly. I mean, perhaps it *is* all Rosy, and all I can say is that in that case Rosy is my heroine and my bride. The only girl I've ever stuck with.

Oh God, this isn't what you came for, is it? Pathetic old buffer after all, baring what passes for his soul. It's just that – you're practically the only Welsh woman I've ever met, you know that? And now I'm hanging all this round your lovely neck, turning you into God knows what, some sort of bloody *sacrament.*

VALERIE [*hesitates; then*]: I do need to go, actually. I've got to meet Michael. Is it all right if I, if I come again? Quite soon?

DAVID: It's not fair really. You didn't get to have tea made with your – what did you call, it, kettle? [*Cheering up a bit.*] You should come and see what happens when the cauldron boils over. Do you know that's what happens in –

VALERIE: No, love, I don't know [*kisses his cheek*]. You can tell me; next time.

[*She leaves. PETRA comes in again, behind DAVID.*]

PETRA [*quietly*]: There's a sod of a war on. Still. Yes? [*Pause.*] No armistice for you.

DAVID: Do you remember when I said once, if only the war had gone on a bit longer I might have learned how to do parades and things, and you said –

PETRA: I said the people of Europe weren't going to thank you for prolonging the war just so you could learn to tie your bootlaces.

[*They smile.*]

DAVID: It's what I live in. The trenches. It's a matter of life and death there whether the words connect or not. Do you wonder I miss it? Even if it's waiting for another bullet, another bayonet in the back. Nightfall and no-one coming. And the noises from all the other buggers waiting with their insides leaking out.

Waiting for the word that changes things. The effing word.
The Efficacious Word.

[*Silence. Blackout.*]

Scene II

[*Plainsong* (Salve Regina) as *lights come up. Compline is finishing. ERIC to front.*]

ERIC: It's where it bolts together, like a good mortice joint: coming together at the end of the day, laying it all down in the right place, and then – you're free. In monasteries you don't talk after Compline. Did I tell you I thought once we should try and do that here? [*PETRA comes into view behind him.*] Just silence, laid over everything like a fall of snow [*starts rolling a cigarette*].

PETRA: And the world made new and everything stowed away under the white carpet. I do see how that works, I really do. I just can't believe you ever thought you and the rest could actually shut up for that long, specially last thing at night. [*ERIC laughs uneasily.*] Actually I'm not being funny. I don't see how *anyone* manages that sort of silence for long. Snow melts fast. [*Edgily.*] It's not as though you can just tell your mind or your memory to close down, is it?

ERIC: Come on, Petra, no point in sulking. The past's the past, yes? What more is there to say? [*Pause.*] I want to know how things are with you two. Have you heard from him?

PETRA: David? Or Denis?

ERIC [*laughs*]: What a thing, eh? Two young men after you. Who's a lucky girl?

PETRA [*quiet*]: Not me. [*Pause.*] David's not said anything; Denis says he'll marry me as soon as I've said no to Dai. What do I do, Pa?

ERIC: Well. [*Pause.*] You know we'll be away in France for a fortnight, me and Mummy, from next Wednesday. Sort it before we get back, will you?

PETRA: I thought – I thought you wanted Dai and me to.... When he first came and you seemed to think he was the one to...to take it all off you, only without anyone moving away. And then Father John and the betrothal thing in chapel, and the ring – this ring with the quote from the Song of Songs. You wanted it, didn't you, me and Dai? You wanted it, and I wanted you to have it.

ERIC: You wanted *me* to.... You just seemed – well, natural together then. I thought you knew what was good for you, to tell you the truth.

PETRA: Pa. I was nineteen, for Christ's sake. And it's not as if I'd been – mixing with lots of men over the years.

[*Silence; awkward. ERIC shifts around irritably.*]

ERIC: Well. After all...well, *he* seemed to know what was good for him, too. Hair-trigger reactions, he said [*imitates DAVID's hesitant manner*], very, um, responsive to, er, women. So yes, I thought, why not, makes sense. And now he just bloody drifts everywhere, buggers off to the monastery for a couple of months. Can't make anything of the stuff he's doing, and he seems to have forgotten anything I ever taught him. If he ever really listened, which I doubt. That's it, I suppose. He's like a lot of people who look weak; core of solid steel when it's their ideas or their, I don't know, [*sarcastic*] *creativity* at stake. One thing I do know, he won't be told. I mean, don't get me wrong here. I love him. He's a sweet man, no malice, no dramas or tantrums. No ambition, I think sometimes. Except to be his own man in his work. Well, good luck to him, I say. But it's not what we do here.

PETRA: I think he's the most ambitious man I know. No, that's not right. He wouldn't give a damn if he never got a review in the papers or a single exhibition. It's just that he knows there's one job he has to do. He just doesn't know what it looks like yet.

ERIC: No, no, no. That's balls. Art-nonsense, romantic bullshit, mystical creative vocations and all the rest of that garbage. I used to think he could resist all that. But he still talks to those silly bastards in London, all those art school types, and he gets flattered by all those characters like Nicholson and Ede. Tell you the truth, you'd be well out of that. Can't see you being part of all that game, Artist's Wife, making the tea while they talk about significant bloody form and post-effing-Impressionism.

PETRA: Completely different from making the tea while they talk about Thomas Aquinas, of course. All right, all right, I know what you mean, sort of. I'm afraid of that too, of being the stupid woman who can't talk but backs up her man in the great sodding war of artistic struggle. [*Pause.*] You're saying don't, aren't you? You're saying Denis.

ERIC: Your life, Pet. Really. Mind you –

PETRA [*laughs briefly*]: Don't pretend. You can't let go, can you? [*Beat.*] Denis says can he come again after Christmas.

ERIC [*impatient*]: All *right*. Let him. If he asks, say yes. There; permission enough?

PETRA: You know Dai talked to him. Actually *talked* to him, in London, when he was back with his parents. Couldn't understand why Denis was so stand-offish, he said. God, poor

Dai. Sometimes I think he shouldn't be allowed out alone. He makes me feel as if I was fifty, some sort of raddled old tart. And then he talks to me as if I were a virgin martyr who'd be horrified to know where children came from. God. And then you, you talk as though, as though....

ERIC [*lowers voice*]: That's enough, now. We are not going over it again. All right: we...I know it had – I knew it had to stop, so...I mean it's not as though you were – well – I mean there wasn't, it wasn't as though there was *harm* done. Sort of a game really, nothing I'm proud of, all right, but I –

PETRA: Harm? Who to?

ERIC: Christ, Petra. You know what I...

PETRA: To you? Never mind me, that's my business. But you, what about you, was there *harm*, as you call it, harm to your *soul*, for God's sake, because if there wasn't I don't know what anything, anything... [*silence*].

ERIC: It's a vale of tears, sweetheart, just like we've been singing about. Exile. Poor banished children of Eve. We never get it right. That's what the Church is for, scrubbing up when it's all gone wrong and getting the map straight again so you can see where you're going. And I'm off to bed. So should you be. [*Pause.*] You'll be fine. He'll be – [*not quite sure, shrugs*] fine. [*Kisses PETRA awkwardly on the cheek.*] Night, love.

PETRA: Night, Pa.

[*He leaves. She wanders towards the front. During the following, DAVID comes in slowly, comes alongside her.*].

Simple as that. "Scrubbing up." God.
    So much not to say; not now; all over with; never really a problem. I never told Dai, of course. I think he was a bit shocked sometimes by – by what I was, well, ready to do

97

with him; what I knew about, I suppose. Not really suburban Brockley, I imagine, not what nice girls understood about. But how do you say it without changing everything?

And all that time, I didn't want it to change. It's easy to say now, well, it was him who was dithering and I never forced him to the point. But it *was* me too. Like Penelope – keep weaving and perhaps you'll never have to make up your mind. The hours I spent on that loom. [*To DAVID*] They were really bloody freezing, those winters at Capel, weren't they? Just as well you had my three-inch thick trousers to keep you warm. It wasn't so bad in Sussex.

DAVID: It wasn't so bad in Sussex. [*Laughs.*] My God, there's a line for you! The whole crisis of modern civilisation in - what? Six, seven words. Comment for all occasions of distress. It was good, though, to start with, of course it was.

[*Lights change, DAVID and PETRA join hands and stroll downstage, back in Sussex.*]

DAVID: Walk?

PETRA: You mean run. You trot on ahead talking and I stumble along falling over my feet in the grass. Really not fair. It's not even as though you had longer legs than mine.

DAVID: Sorry. But you do get me talking. Just by being along. [*Pause.*] I thought we might have a walk to the, er, the usual place....

PETRA [*touches his face*]: Don't think there's time, love; and I've got a singing practice in half an hour and I don't want to arrive looking as if I've been tumbling in the hay. Even if I have.

DAVID: All right, then, old wife, no private time today; occasions of sin postponed due to, um, unfriendly geography.

[*They lean against each other; no hurry.*] How long have you all been here now?

PETRA: Ages. Can't really remember anywhere else; I can't have been more than two when we moved. But here specifically, must be, oh, ten years, eleven. And Betty and Joan, they're the same: Sussex feels like home. But it's funny in a way. Feels like home, but the family gets further and further away from everyone else; people in the village looking at us, and it feels as if they don't really like what they see. And I worry about the community too; you know, all the rows Pa gets into with the others. I don't know, it's a bit of a feeling of – sort of slowly pulling away from the shore on this little boat, just Pa and Mummy and us, not knowing anything much except what the parents are telling us – well, Pa mostly, obviously. And everything on board is natural, that's the way things are and have to be, nothing to worry about, nothing to ask questions about that don't have an answer. An answer from Pa. Full of answers, Pa. I think – no, I don't know. Oh, just that he seems to be sort of digging himself in more, nothing else makes any impact. He chisels away at his own world....

[*Pause; she walks a little distance away.*]

You know he's talking about a move some time? [*DAVID shakes his head.*] Things aren't too good just now. He's sort of – I don't know: run into something, inside, outside, he can't.... He hates that, hates it when people don't just – get themselves into shape for him.

[*Pause.*]

All our lessons have been at home, you know, always. Wonderful in some ways, we've all learned to *do* things, carve, spin, cook, we read the right books, Pa even tried to teach us Latin. Nothing to go outside for.

DAVID: Didn't you play with other children?

PETRA: Well, not a lot. There were the other children here, bit older. Hardly ever children from the village or anywhere outside. Visitors' families now and then. But yes. I did sometimes think, how odd, not everyone does things like we do. Tell you one thing I remember, when I was really tiny. One of the visitors' children arrived with a doll – you know, a doll with lots of artificial hair and red spots on her cheeks and nice dresses, and my God, I wanted that doll as I've never wanted anything since.

   I asked Pa could I have a doll. I must have been – don't know – four or five? He'd always say how he loved children and the child's view of the world and how he approved of toys. You know how he goes on about children's art and all that. He just didn't approve of nasty commercial toys, lovely wicked bourgeois toys like that doll, toys that actual children have. I'll make you a doll, he said; and he did.

   I've still got it. I was so excited he was going to make something just for me. And there it was, as if he'd looked up a dictionary definition of a doll and never looked at an actual one that children play with. It's like one of those statues, where are they? Easter Island. Or some sort of [*slight giggle*] tribal fetish. All wood, of course, handcarved. Torso, two straight little arms you could move, two straight little legs, no neck, round head, hair carved on. The kind of doll you'd stick pins into if you were a witch, Betty said; really helpful, that was. All right, yes, I cried a bit on my own after he gave it to me. He meant to be so – generous, I suppose, and it was all wrong, *all* wrong, all wrong, he means to be... but it isn't... [*struggles a bit with this*]. Not that you can talk. Remember those puppets you carved, just a few months after you arrived? I thought they looked like traitors' heads on Tower Bridge or wherever. And then you told me they were supposed to be me and Betty and Joan and Gordian: my God, I thought, what sort of monster is this? [*Half-laugh; pause.*]

DAVID: Does he really not love children, then? I always thought....

PETRA [*wipes face, shakes head to clear*]: He loves the idea of children. He loves – *fertility*. I sometimes think he can't see the point of real live children, though. He knows you've got to give them time to play and all the rest of it, but he's always looking at the clock. Time they got *on* with things. Give the child a doll if she wants one, but let her know that dolls are things you drop as soon as you can.

DAVID: "They can bloody well wait for the stretcher-wallahs."

DAVID and PETRA [*in unison*]: "Don't you know there's a sod of a war on."

[*They laugh together, then silence for a moment, then they stroll away out of the light.*]

Scene III

[*VALERIE and PETRA, both facing audience; VALERIE seated by a table, speaking on the phone.*]

VALERIE: Yes, I know, love. Yes. You know sometimes I wish I could talk to Petra before I tell him. Yes, I know she's still around, but I'd be scared out of my knickers to meet her. No. No, he'll be – oh Christ, I was going to say he'll be all right, but he won't really. He'll live, like he has so far. There was – I hadn't realised properly, I mean I sort of knew about her, there was this woman, Prudence something. Yes, yes. Yes, he was – pretty much obsessed with her, I think: very upper-class English by the sound of it, and then she went off and lived with someone else and then he died and she died. Yes, I know. No, it was, oh something like multiple sclerosis, I think? But I don't know, for David it was some sort of confirmation nothing was going to work, ever. No. He talks about her as if she'd been like him, a great damaged soul, war casualty, struck down by melancholy and so on. You know, drifting out to sea on a boat without oars, with her arms spread out. Well, he lived, somehow, he went on. Yes. It's just that – no, I know, but – no, that's right, that's right, only he – yes, it's as though something just gave way, just *went* somewhere along the line. Yes, yes. Yes, it's felt like we're friends, and I'm really scared of spoiling. No, of course not, get away! Well, all right, yes, nearly once, I think I just felt so sorry. Yes, but what I wonder is – no, what I wonder is whether she felt like this,

Petra, I mean, whether there was just too much to cope with, too much to – carry, I suppose. Yes, well, she was a Catholic, I guess that must have – Eric? no, never. No, he sounds pretty frightening. Mm. Mm, yes... [*fades as she stands up to stretch her legs*].

PETRA: And where would she start, I wonder? Nice talkative woman, sporty, sexy, Welsh; you can see what a lifeline she seems. Like poor Prudence, only with a proper Welsh pedigree.

It's a good question, what did I feel? And what would we have to say to each other, her and me, Prudence and me, Prudence and her? Different planets. What does she imagine, I wonder? Poor little peasant girl, weighed down with religion and frightened of complicated people like Dai; thank God she found someone normal to rescue her. Or: poor little thing, famous father, never lived up to his expectations, looking for a quiet life with the kids and the washing machine. [*Laughs briefly.*] Pa would have burst a blood vessel if I'd bought a washing machine; pretty much on the level of condoms in his book.

[*Looks at VALERIE.*] There I am, sitting in her mind, in the corner, saying nothing; still clinging to Dai like a cobweb...

VALERIE: ...because I can't imagine really, stuck in Capel-y-ffin – what? Oh, it's up beyond Abergavenny, back of beyond. Yes, stuck with this mad father and all those artists and priests. What kind of woman would *you* be? No, that's right. Yes; yes. I think they were all petrified of real Welsh people, mind you; like David, bless him. Overflowing with all this stuff from the Middle Ages and King Arthur and still can't order a cup of tea in Welsh. No, don't, love, no, that's not it. No, I do actually...yes, I love him. Really. But what do you do, eh? What *do* you do? Yes, I know it sounds stale or bloody obvious, but – yes, it's like the bullet's still in there. Wounded, that's the word. When he talks about

Mametz Wood, you know.... Yes, First World War, seems like the Middle Ages, doesn't it? But he gets right back into it sometimes, when things are, I don't know, when things are sort of closing in? And he'll tell these... [*moves away*].

PETRA: Ah. Yes, she's been listening. And she's not stupid, she can do a bit of diagnosing. I wonder if she's guessed anything else.

Probably not. How would she? I do still go over it sometimes, you know, not a lot but sometimes. Should I ever have said yes to him? And then should I have said no? When I look back, I can't remember what I was actually *feeling*, which is so stupid when you think about it. But all I can imagine is that both times round it was like making a last jump to solid land when the water's rising all around you. And when you've jumped you're so out of breath and so sort of shocked you don't notice anything else for a bit.

Jumping to get away from Pa, or to get as far away as looked possible. Not very far actually, and he was half-pushing me in any case. So I didn't notice who Dai really was and what he could and couldn't do, and then it was all – well, like the weaving when I started learning it, threads everywhere, and heavy material and heavy machines, or like the bedclothes winding round you in a dream and it's all just too bloody *heavy* to get off.

You know when that's happening and you're half-asleep and you just have to make this massive effort to wake up and your heart pounds but you somehow push through. That was what it was, when Denis came along and I decided that was it, that was it, I couldn't go on with it all. And there I was, gasping, heart racing, not sure if I was asleep or awake; couldn't see or hear anyone else. And everyone telling me how calm I was with it all; my God, I must be such a bloody brilliant actress. I didn't let myself think about Dai really, not for months, not for years, I suppose, even when he – I never told anybody at the time, but six months before the wedding he asked me, really begged me, to drop Denis and, well, give it another try. And he sounded desperate, and I must have been so bloody arctic, I still couldn't see him or hear him, I knew it was too risky. It was like watching him through frosted glass, bleeding slowly and his mouth opening and shutting. Now that I remember it, I think it must have been like it was for him in the War, deafening noise everywhere and watching someone's mouth opening and shutting and knowing they were bleeding to death and not being able to do a thing.

I suppose that was him trying to jump. Only where to?

VALERIE: ...Not really, no; no. It's not going to be easy. But you need to understand, he's so – I mean I can't just let go of him, he's so *lovely,* he's so, well, exciting to be with. Yes, I *am* serious. You feel somebody's steering you round this landscape that you'll never really get hold of but you want to. I know he doesn't know a thing about politics. No, I talk to him about Plaid Cymru's economic policy and my moments of glory doing athletics for Wales in the stadium in Cardiff, and he comes back with Gruffydd ab yr Ynad Coch's lament for Llywelyn the Last. No, I know: struggling to pronounce it properly, bless him. But still. You want to – oh, I don't know, make him feel safe. Breaks your heart, really. [*Faces front alongside PETRA.*]

PETRA [*turns to look at her briefly*]: Well yes; if you let it. [*Forward a little.*] I just don't think she has to jump anywhere, even if she is a champion athlete. Can't see her choking in a dream really. Dai's not her daily routine, he's not round every corner; she's got a safe man lined up all the time. My God, I bet David will hate him. For a few weeks anyway. But she knows a bit of it, she knows how much you can give without getting drowned in it all. Bless her. It won't be the same as it was with me. He'll be grateful, he knows nothing would ever really have happened, not even if they'd properly got together on that terrible old sofa. No. I know what I did. And maybe

I saved his life as well as mine, whatever life he's managed. The trouble is, no one can ever tell you for sure, can they? No one can ever tell you.

[*They turn very briefly to one another, then walk away in opposite directions. Blackout.*]

Scene IV

[*DAVID's room in Harrow. He and VALERIE sitting in silence; DAVID has been drinking. In what follows, VALERIE should be working hard to keep an emotional distance.*]

VALERIE: But you must have guessed –

DAVID [*abruptly, overlapping*]: No. [*Pause.*] Yes of course I bloody did. Christ. Do you know what you've done? Christ.

VALERIE: I told you, when we first met, I told you Michael was –

DAVID: I don't want to hear about fucking Michael. I don't want to hear about you. Why the hell did you come? Don't you see, don't you bloody *see*, we can't go on being friends.

VALERIE [*effort at controlling herself*]: It does *not* have to be like this. It's not as though I'd kept anything back. You *knew* Michael had proposed. I know what sort of things it reopens for you –

DAVID: Oh you do, do you? You do, do you? Christ, why did I ever tell you anything? Why can't you see it's *over*, for God's sake, it's all *over*, all over. [*Silence.*]
    I loved you, do you know that? I really truly loved you. You sit there, pretending to be so calm and, and *adult*, as if we'd just had a little fling and now we could get back to the routine, but don't you see, don't you...see, there isn't a

routine for me, there isn't an ordinary, and you, you'll just go off with him and have a nice normal life in suburban bloody Cardiff, doing nice worthwhile things for the BBC and Plaid Cymru and, and the Women's Institute, for all I know, but I haven't got anything to go back to and Christ I'm frightened, can't you see, I'm frightened, I'm frightened....

VALERIE [*at a loss; gets up, moves around room, fidgets with things, picks up whisky bottle, etc., then, with an effort*]: Look. Don't get me wrong. [*DAVID groans.*] I knew you... loved me; if you'd wanted, if you'd really wanted me – if you'd really wanted me and – well, I'd have.... Oh Christ, I don't know. But you, you were always talking about why it wasn't for you and why – I mean I've never understood this Catholic thing anyway –

DAVID [*tearful*]: You really don't understand it, do you? It's not "this Catholic thing." It's this David thing. This thing here on the sofa, the sofa where you kissed me and I thought for a moment it might happen, God, it just might happen, do you remember that? and I know, well of course I know it didn't and all right it couldn't perhaps, I don't know what I'm saying, do I? And you don't seem to mind, you just don't seem to mind and you talk about *reopening* things as if you understood what it's like being adrift without sails and mast and oars and the fog closing in. Like being alone in the wood again. Fog. Noises. [*Begins to shake.*] And now here we are again; "walking in the morning on the flat roof of the world." I said that, didn't I? I wrote it in that poem you never understood, you never really tried to read it, did you? Did you?

VALERIE: For God's *sake*, David. [*Pause; she rubs her forehead.*] Just think about it all for a moment, will you? I was really glad, I was so bloody glad to have you as a friend. And I'm sorry, it was my fault, I let you think it could be something else. But I loved it, you were so lovely, you were so

– full of things, all the things you loved and wanted to share, but you *knew* about Michael, you knew what was going to happen. Don't spoil it all now, don't spoil it with Michael. He wants to come and see you, you know. [*DAVID shakes his head violently.*] You can do this.

[*DAVID sits with eyes closed. Pause.*]

DAVID: You made me lovely. You made me want to share things. You made me feel the connections, feel the waters rushing together under the ground, all those streams woven in and running into the sea. You made me – joyful. Stupid bloody word, sort of word you only use in church. Only word I can find. Joy. Something running over, pouring out.

[*Raises whisky glass and deliberately spills it on carpet. VALERIE tuts, produces handkerchief and mops some of it up.*]

There we go, you see? you can soak up the joy with a little lace hanky and no-one will ever know it was there.

VALERIE: This is no good, David. I'll come back when you've had a bit of time. You need to know that I'm not going to let all this disappear. I want you for a friend, you do bloody know that, don't you? When you've stopped feeling sorry for yourself, you'll manage, I know you will. No, just shut up now; there's nothing sensible to say at the moment, not for either of us. I'll go now, all right? I'll give you a ring before the weekend. All right? [*Insistently.*] All right?

DAVID [*muffled, tearful again*]: All right.

VALERIE: God, I hate this. I hate leaving you like this. But you know we can't talk about it now, right? We just can't. You need to think a bit, that's all.

[*She gets up; turns back as if to kiss goodbye, hesitates and grasps his shoulder, avoids his hand as it comes up to grab hers, leaves. PETRA comes in upstage, wanders down to stand behind sofa, hands on D's shoulders. Silence for a moment.*]

PETRA [*neutrally*]: Oh dear.

DAVID [*sits upright, slowly, pushes his hands through his hair; still a bit rickety from the drink*]: Oh dear. Indeed.

PETRA: All the clichés. Call yourself a writer.

DAVID: I know. I know. So bloody humiliating. You have this emotion grabbing you in the guts and the privates, and you just come out with all the second-rate, hand-me-down, porcelain-ducks-on-the-wall standard fittings for The End of the Affair [*signals capital letters*]. Terrible book called something like that, isn't there? All about the hound of heaven or some such. Not the kind of thing your Pa would have any time for. And you think, there's Auden or Eliot or some brilliant bugger or other saying you have the most sophisticated modernist sensibility in Britain and you can only say these stupid self-pitying things. And do the drink stuff as well. Whisky with tears. Just a splash for me, please. Was I always as stupid as that?

PETRA: I think the popular vote at Capel was that you could do a good line in subdued self-pity. With a sweet long-suffering smile. You know, when we were in Sussex, there'd always be people passing through for a night or two with problems of one kind or another, and we used to call them the Sorrowful Mysteries of the Rosary? I used to think of you like that, sometimes: Sorrowful Mystery. Sorry. Can't say I blame you, though.

DAVID: Did I talk to you about what it was like then, at the start? About the war and all that?

PETRA: Not a lot really. Not quite what it was *like*, anyway. Plenty of stories, like how you were shot; you used to recycle them a fair bit, you know. Not a lot else.

DAVID: Just as well.

PETRA: Just as well. You will see her again, won't you?

DAVID: Oh yes, I think so. I'll send them a nice wedding present. What do you give people these days? Napkin-rings? Egg-cosies? Napkin-cosies? I really wanted to try and paint her, you know. Not quite the moment, is it?

PETRA: Might be. I see your point, though. No, I didn't believe all that stuff about it being over. You do survive, you know.

DAVID: Oh yes; for what it's worth. I can remember the poor sods hanging on the barbed wire, like old clothes hung up for sale; alive, some of them, alive for maybe a day or so. Survivors. It all comes back to that, though, doesn't it? A man hung up in public, dying. Don't get me wrong, don't think I'm getting a Christ-complex. It's just that I suppose *he* hangs up there because that's where we all are, one way or another. Dying, surviving. Waiting. And the only thing I've got to do is keep my eyes on that and wait to see if the lines really do come together there, if that's the shape of the whole story and the shape of the land and the sea, so that it's all changed because it's all one thing, one picture, from the start of everything to the end. And there's nowhere else to start from except what's – hanging on the wire. Look long enough and maybe it starts looking like something else; like a tree pushing up, or something.

It's a two-edged thing, you know, this roof of the world business. You walk along as if there was nothing solid around or under or alongside, but you know, you just know that the lines are weaving together, you can hear them humming in the fog, in the quiet. Lines making for you, a bullet slowly heading at you, slow, really slow, takes all day, like a dream or a slow-motion film. And it's so terrifying, because you don't know if you can – carry it all, hold it....

Do you remember that day when we were walking once, and I told you I couldn't feel my feet touching the ground? It was just like something that happened once in the trenches, when I was supposed to be crossing one of those duckboards to another gun emplacement, and I couldn't move. It was as if I was hanging above the earth with my feet just mechanically swinging, nothing behind or in front, and absolute, utter panic inside. Not even Mametz was that bad.

The doctor gave me a tonic; bloody wonderful what doctors can do.

PETRA: Was that when you stopped going out? I can remember that spell at Capel when you wouldn't even go to Abergavenny. Dangerous place, of course, Abergavenny. The Passchendaele of North Monmouthshire.

DAVID [*smiles*]: Full of enemy troops. I know. But that's what it felt like, all those silent Welsh locals watching me, calculating the range of a shot or a shell. Bullets humming slowly towards me. Bloody ridiculous, but that's what it was. I felt a fool all the time, really all the time, curled up in bed, and you were so patient, bringing me soup and tea and soft-boiled eggs and all the rest. Only...that moment when I couldn't feel things...that was when I sort of knew again what I had to do, that I just couldn't stop trying to get it down or get it cut into something. Messing around all day long with those engraving tools; it was as though pushing that little burin in to the copper was pushing into the soil, planting something. Or...chipping away and watching a face appear as the dust falls off. And if you don't stay with it all day long and all night long, it goes away again. Don't know how I slept.

PETRA: Pa said it was like having a new baby in the house. Not a compliment from him, really.

DAVID: No. He never thought it was Work with a capital W. Even if I couldn't stop. God, it was a bad couple of months, that. And then, stone me, off he goes with all the others to bloody *France* because it was so cold, and it was just us, and you told me to go back to my parents for a bit. The miraculous healing powers of suburban life.

PETRA: So you knew then? I mean you knew where we were – headed?

DAVID: Didn't let myself know. When you told me, it was – well, it was the bullet in the leg again, the great bloody beam swinging round and knocking you over in the wet filth. That's always been my trouble: don't let myself know. I didn't let myself know about Valerie. And then I get so furious with her because I know quite well, I really do, that I was never, absolutely never in a thousand bloody years, going to go to bed with her or marry her or anything. You feel for something and it's not there, you know it isn't there but you think maybe, just perhaps, just this time. And it all...falls away, falls apart. *A, Domine Deus.*

PETRA: Mm?

DAVID: Jeremiah. "Ah Lord God!" When he shouts at God because God's made him what he is and there's no way of actually *being* what he is, doing what he's meant to do, what he's *for*. As your Pa might put it.

PETRA: So what did he say? God, I mean, not Pa. I can sometimes tell the difference.

DAVID: The usual.

PETRA: "Unknown at this address"?

DAVID: Something like that. Just leaves you looking at the wire, usually; there's nothing else for him to say. Or he says, like someone telling you a joke, you know, someone who really can't tell jokes, he says, oh well, if you don't get it, you don't get it. Sort of huffy. [*Pause; then slowly and quite loud.*] *A, a, a Domine Deus.*

[*Blackout.*]

Scene V

[*DAVID at workbench; PETRA comes in carrying a large and clumsily made doll.*]

PETRA: All right to interrupt?

DAVID: Yes of course, love. What on earth have you got there?

PETRA: You did say you wanted to see it. The unique non-commercial doll.

DAVID: This is it, then?

PETRA: Yes; you see what I mean.

DAVID: My God, yes. Pure Eric, isn't it? Distilled essence of human figurine. Still, he meant it kindly.

PETRA: Mm. [*Pause.*] Not even Pa can quite ignore the fact that there's such a thing as being a little girl. [*Shivers.*] Ugh; didn't mean that, quite.

DAVID: Darling? What?

PETRA: What indeed? Don't bother about it. There it is, anyway. [*Pause.*] What are you actually like with children, Dai? I've seen you with the Pepler kids, they like you, even if they haven't got a clue what to make of you. Seems a common reaction.

DAVID [*not very successfully trying to make light of it*]: Oh, I'm just scared of everyone, specially children. You're not, are you? You don't ever seem frightened of anyone.

PETRA: Pa sometimes says that's because I don't have any deep feelings. You know how he goes on. Mind you, that's probably a compliment from his point of view, once he gets on his high horse about sentimental bollocks in art and religion and the rest. Perhaps he thinks I'm a nice restful person to have around because I don't bruise or...bleed too much. Perhaps this thing is really supposed to be a portrait. It looks about as much like me as those bloody awful heads of us that you did.

DAVID: Ah, but it shouldn't just....

PETRA: Yes, I know. It's not meant to look like me. It's Petra under the form of wood or paint or whatever. Is that right? It's just that Petra under the form of flesh and blood feels a bit left out sometimes.

DAVID [*a bit nervous*]: Well, I should be able to do something about that in due course.

PETRA: What about now, Dai? What about now? [*Moves closer.*]

DAVID: Oh Christ. You know I want to.

PETRA: Do I? How I am I supposed to know?

[*Awkward; they don't move. DAVID takes the doll from PETRA and looks at it, moving its arms and legs.*]

PETRA [*sharply*]: No! No, stop it, Dai, stop it, stop it, put the bloody thing down, put it down. [*Pause.*] No, sorry, sorry, ignore me. Sorry.

[*She puts her hands to cheeks, takes a deep breath. DAVID hands the doll back in silence. PETRA looks at it and very deliberately drops it on the ground. DAVID embraces her clumsily; she leans against him, then puts a hand to his chest and pushes him gently away. They look at each other silently.*]

PETRA: You know about archaeology, don't you, Dai? Someone told me once what it's like on a real dig in Egypt or Syria or somewhere: you think this is it, you've got to the bottom, and something just nudges up out of the sand and you know there's more and it – doesn't want to stay buried. And you get a little brush of feathers or something and dust away at what's sticking out, so, so gently, until you see what it is and then you can label it and put it in a big tray ready for the museum.

You could leave that doll there on the path, and the soil and the mud and the goose shit would drift over it for a few hundred years, and then someone might come and brush it all away, very gently, and wonder what it meant, what strange religious cult would use these little images to worship or conjure with or, or, I don't know, jerk around like puppets to give oracles....

DAVID: They dig trenches, don't they, archaeologists? Nasty places, trenches.

PETRA: Mm. Nasty places.

[*They stand holding hands. Light fades, spot on doll on the ground. Then blackout.*]

Scene VI

[*Light up on* DAVID *and* VALERIE *motionless, looking together at the doll on the ground; they move away slowly,* DAVID *sits on the sofa.*]

VALERIE: Well; bit calmer today, then.

DAVID: Oh Christ. I'm so embarrassed, I, um, I must have, I never really know what's going to come up out of the mud, I'm, honestly, I'm sorry, love, I'm so...it must have....

VALERIE: Shh, *cariad*. Doesn't matter. No-one died. [*pause*] Stretcher-wallahs arrived safely, yes?

DAVID [*slowly*]: You know, when...when Petra...when Petra decided she, you know, couldn't, well, couldn't go through with it, I thought to start with, I thought – she never exactly... well, explained it, she just...she sort of said, I'm sure you know this is what you really want. And I could have screamed at her, *For Christ's sake!* What gives you the right to say what I want, eh? What gives you the right to.... Took me days to stop shaking, crying, all the rest. Not to mention a message from bloody Eric via somebody or other, all sort of, "Great shame and so on, but it's better for everyone in the long run, eh?"

This is what you really want, she said. And eventually, when all the noise was over, I had to ask that, ask, Was she right? Was she right?

Yes and no. I did want her, oh Christ I wanted her; at night when I was itching all over with, you know.... And in the workshop; just somebody to turn round to and smile and get on. All that. More.

[*VALERIE sits down beside him.*]

And then – well you know what I said about being shot? You don't realise until you clock that the wet stuff in your shoes is blood. First thing I thought was the bloody obvious: yes, it's like being shot, the big thump and not knowing what's hit you and not being able to walk or move anything. Only it was – it was as if the shot had been years before, and I'd only just noticed the blood. The letter she wrote, that wasn't it, that wasn't the shot. I'd had blood trickling down into my shoes all the time I was with her, years and bloody years. Because that was when...that was when I couldn't move. And I knew she was right. Somewhere deep down I didn't want it, something was already, I don't know, taken away, paralysed. My psychiatrist had a field day with all that, I can tell you. But they're so...so bloody simple-minded, psychiatrists. I knew – I knew – [*pause*].

Bear with me, love...I knew what I wanted was the wound. All right, prize for pretentious rubbish. But I knew something had been sort of opened up in the trenches, something I couldn't close without closing up, well, everything that mattered. And I had to...you know; just *live* there. I had to lie in the forest and wait. Lie where the bodies were stacked on top of each other all through the hundreds of years. Lie in the troughs where they throw the seeds and heap the soil on. Where the rats live and the wire, and the, the, can't say it...the whatever it is that sleeps under it all. I had to live there. In the trench. With the roof above. And all the little roots and filaments and curls and grips of vegetation joining everything up, bit by bit, but you don't know what's going to break the surface. And, well, going to bed with Petra, having kids, making money or whatever, and a house and a washing machine, it just felt...it felt like climbing out and closing it up and, well...*no*, all I could say was *no*....

VALERIE: So that's what she heard you saying? That you were in love with the trenches after all?

DAVID: Must have been. How do you get to say what you don't know you know? Is that why people write poems and things? But I don't know how she knew, how she – heard. What was really inside her. I couldn't ever....

[*PETRA to the front, lit.*]

PETRA: Well, no one could, ever, it seems.

Thing is, we didn't really have any way of talking about it then. We might have been living on the moon most of the time, no idea, no idea at all, of what other families were like. Nothing to judge Pa by.

So we didn't – didn't judge him, I mean. Everyone wants us to now. Do I? I suppose I do. When I think objectively about it, I think, that man controlled my childhood and took away things that could have made it happy. That man made me see more than ever I wanted or understood about, about men, some men anyway. That man got hold of my mind and my body and turned it where he wanted. Should I be angrier than I am?

But it did mean that I could see with Dai there was something that was never going to work. Two people bleeding quietly and waiting for the ambulances.

And even then, I kept Denis waiting for three years. Just learning to breathe again. Weaving away like Penelope. Letting the light change, letting the landscape shift a bit.

I can remember when I was about sixteen, Betty took me for a walk. And she wasn't like herself, she didn't have much to say and then she gave me a cigarette, very grown-up, and she said, "Has he been talking to you?" and I said,

"Who?" and she said, "You know" and I did, because he'd been – talking about what happened with men and women and how wonderful it was, and how he was going to show me wonderful things, and then, well, yes, showing me things, showing me.... And Betty said, "Does he poke you about?" And I said, "Well, yes, a bit, but isn't that...?" And she was very quiet for a bit and said: "You mustn't let him, you know? You just mustn't let him." And then she walked away very fast, and she never talked about it again.

Let him, I thought? As if he ever asked permission. As if I knew I had a choice. Not very helpful, but that was Betty.

Hard to believe, isn't it? And I knew Dai was supposed to be the one who'd take me off Pa's hands for good and sort it all out so that there'd be grandchildren and all the rest, and sometimes I was cross that I was just being packed up and handed over. Only I knew Dai wasn't really going to do the job. And yes, that was sort of comforting. He didn't just think, Oh, there's a woman, I know what *she's* for. I never said anything to him. I didn't know if he ever even started guessing, guessing there was *something* anyway. But at least he looked down there, into the dark bits where things lie and rot or sprout or whatever. And somehow it was all right with him to sit and sort of not *try* for a bit.

[*DAVID to front, lit.*]

DAVID: How do you guess a thing like that? I knew she knew more than she should – no, that's not right, but you know what I mean? About, well, bodies, men's bodies, you know.... But how can you think...? So I didn't.

You know, doing all those paintings and carvings of her: when you know all that you've left out, every time, you know, you just know this art business can't be just a *job,* just a making of some sort of sophisticated tool. Bearing witness, that's what it is, like in the nineteenth century, you write a letter and then you'd write across what you'd written as if you were weaving, making a net, a – what, a web, something tight enough to hold all the – all the debris, all the dropped things and people waiting to hear their real names being called, waiting to be taken to some sort of home. Even if it can't work. Even if *you* can't get it all home, carry this net of struggling gasping *stuff*. Never finishing, never sealing it off and saying, That's the job. Still bleeding somewhere, like the bodies on the wire.

[*ERIC to front, lit.*]

ERIC: All right, we get things wrong. The chisel slips, you cut the nose or the hand off by mistake, you think this is all right and it isn't, and you know it isn't. I did know; well, after a while. It did stop. I mean *I* stopped. Funny how you say "it" when you don't want to admit you got it wrong. It was just, there was always something so indescribable about what goes on down there, when this ridiculous little spigot turns into a flower and a fountain and everything just explodes in joy, why wouldn't you want to do it again and again and let everyone and everything into the secret? But yes, all right, it had to....

They don't seem to have been ruined by it all. Do they? No, really; really. Tough girls, sensible. They never...well they never, they never *reproached* me, is that the word? They never ran away or anything. I mean yes, all right, Petra...she could be strange sometimes, but I thought well, teenage girls, lots going on, they're going to have their strange moments. And yes, all right, it was a mistake to push her at Dai, I suppose, but he seemed to be.... He got the point of some of it, I thought, but what the hell went wrong? Good solid craftsman, then all these peculiar paintings and that bizarre rigmarole about the war. Never really understood why it felt like that for him. Still, if idiots are going to fight bloody mad capitalist wars, that's what you expect. Denis knew how to manage all that; so why didn't Dai, eh?

I mean if it *had* really...hurt, damaged them, you'd expect them to say something, wouldn't you? And they never did, not really. Not really. You know, you make a slip, you get the stroke wrong, and you can *see*: you can see the bits lying on the floor, you can see what's gone missing or what's gone askew. Nothing like that, was there? So all right, admit it was wrong, it was a mistake, get it right next time, don't sit there picking over it and making it more than it was. I think they got that message, they got on with things, they did what they were *for*. [*Pause.*]

Sometimes when I looked at her, I thought, there's nothing left to say to her now. As if I'd put a big stone over the well; no water coming. Nothing from her, nothing from me.

But still, it wasn't as if there were – bits lying on the floor. It wasn't... [*turns away; light on the doll.*]

[*VALERIE to front, lit.*]

VALERIE: Sometimes you dream you've walked on stage in a play where no one's explained the plot and you've never seen the script. I used to find that with David's conversation at first – all that, "You know" and "You remember" about all sorts of things I didn't know the first thing about. The *Gododdin* and King Arthur and Roman legions and English folksongs and the decline of the West. God knows. Booming echoes round my head. But there was something about the, well, the space that made the echoes. You didn't want to leave, there was always going to be something more. And he was so kind, and I felt so sort of protective and grateful all at once. Only – sometimes, you'd look at him and he'd be somewhere fathoms down and there was nothing to say....

And then all that personal stuff, all those people from the Twenties I'd never met or heard of; all the ghosts, or not ghosts but all the voices you'd pick up in his mind, like in a cave, and you'd never know quite what note you might be striking, and he'd always be listening and sort of humming in sympathy. Trying to talk in the middle of that; only so much you can manage.

Oh but I did love him, though. I did. And I think I loved all the rest too because of him, even if I didn't know the story, couldn't make sense of the story. I know what he'd say, too. You can't make sense of anything unless you're making sense of everything. Always more to do, another set of dots to join up.

You'd see it all round you there in that room. The drawings with all the little details, the bits scrubbed out and re-done, the inscriptions with all the extra things round the edges, even the letters he'd be writing, on and on, with the notes in different-coloured ink at the sides and round the top, and the articles he'd never finish.

Out on the water alone, he'd say sometimes, out in this little boat, and scribbling away to find the co-ordinates, to map the whole seascape, and then the fog coming down and the noises you couldn't identify. Always –

DAVID [*forward into spot*]: Always listening. The silence under the gunfire. The breathing body under the soil. The roots where everything knots itself together down there, under the roof you're lying on while the blood runs away and it all rushes through the veins like in a dream when you've got flu and you know, you *know* it's turning round one axle and that, *that's* what you've got to want.

> "He does what is done in many places
> what he does other
> he does after the mode
> of what has always been done."

You listen and you lift it, carefully, not to break anything, and you put it there, on the wire.

[*Picks up the doll and places it on the worktable.*]

And then you lie and wait.

[*Lies on the sofa. The others stand at its sides and head. Blackout.*]

LAZARUS

Lazarus

Rather bad quality recorded voice, as if in church, getting nearer: "I am the Resurrection, and the Life: he that believeth in me, though he were dead, yet shall he live: And whosoever liveth and believeth in me shall never die."

FIRST VOICE

[*Male, middle-aged, walks on, faces audience.*]

"I am the Resurrection and the Life." That's what the vicar read when the coffin came in. Some funerals are tough, this one was. Friend at work, her son crashed his motorbike, two weeks in intensive care, then he died; seventeen. [*Turns, paces.*] You know how you are at funerals sometimes, things sort of come into focus because you can't concentrate too long on what's really going on. So when the vicar walked into the crem chapel, I thought, What the hell's that about? "I am the Resurrection." Who talks like that? Like saying "I am the Coronation" or something. And "the Resurrection and the Life." You say the life *of* something, the life and soul of the party, the life of I don't know, the life of this or that kind of thing, or "life on earth," like the telly programme. So what's with this "*the* Life"?

[*Faces audience.*] I asked the vicar at the door; don't know quite what I said, embarrassing to remember now, but I sort of asked what that stuff meant, the Resurrection and the Life, and he laughed a bit and said, Well, yes, er, it's a bit strange, isn't it? It's the old translation, we use it because people seem to like it at funerals. It's from St John's Gospel, maybe you should look at a modern version, if you're interested I could recommend…and I just said, yeah, OK, thanks, 'cause I couldn't be bothered, and he obviously didn't have an answer. Didn't have a clue what the question was, even. And I could see he was gearing up to have a discussion about this business of translations of the Bible. I'd never realised there was more than one, but I wasn't really interested. Wasn't what I was asking about, so I walked off. [*Moves away, sits.*]

SECOND VOICE

[*Middle-aged, female, light coming up on her, seated, not looking at audience.*]

He kept on asking, "He coming, then?" all the time he was in bed those last few days, and I just went on saying, yes, course he is, he's on his way right now. On the last day, though, he stopped asking. I remember saying, He'll be here soon, I know he'll be here soon, but he didn't seem to be listening by then.

When he came, I ran to him and it all poured out: where the hell were you, where the *hell* were you? Because he kept asking and asking, where were you, is he coming? And he didn't say anything, he stood there and I could see he was shivering and sweating as if he had a temperature or something.

[*Gets up, walks slowly downstage.*]

It's not as if we ever had much in the way of friends. Three people in the house, a widow, a spinster, and an invalid little brother, not much to bring people through the door. When my husband died, I came back. My sister had always stayed to look after him, because he'd had fits since he was little, really frightening, and we sort of always knew that one day there'd be something we couldn't do anything about. She'd got caught, never went out, always in the kitchen or in his room, no boyfriends or anything. And I didn't want to see anyone anyway, not after the accident. Grief makes you ugly. The house was ugly. Too much to manage. Not surprising nobody came. [*Sits again.*]

Only *he* did, just knocking on the door one day with all the rest of his friends and asking if they could sit down for half an hour, and he made us laugh as if we were ordinary and not ugly. Oh God, we wanted him so much those last days. I'll never stop hearing Lazarus saying over and over, "He coming, then?" the words all lumpy and muffled.

Where the hell were you, I shouted. And he stood there, and then he wiped his forehead and just said, "Well, I'm here now. Where are you? Where's he? Where have you buried him?"

FIRST VOICE

[*Light up on him, seated.*]

I looked it up one day, John's Gospel, in a Gideon Bible in a hotel. It was like the vicar'd said, one of these new ones, and it didn't, I don't know, it didn't sound quite the same. I sort of flicked through the pages around, couldn't make head or tail.

When I was clearing out my auntie's house a few months ago, I found her Bible. Big old thing, biggish print, I think it might have been one of those family Bibles, probably from her gran or something. I thought I'd look up this John's thing again. It took me a while to find it, and then – don't know why – I read the first bit out loud.

[*Gets up, moves towards audience.*]

When I was little and I heard thunderstorms I used to think it was like the noise of someone moving big empty wooden boxes around upstairs, and all these heavy things falling over. That's what it reminded me of, heavy stuff falling over in an empty room somewhere. The Word was with God and the Word was God. No idea what it meant. Only the noise of it, big hard boxes falling over slowly on a wood floor.

THIRD VOICE

[*Young, male, walking on slowly and sitting to face audience.*]

He started off with her, walking to the cemetery, shivering as if he had a cold or flu. And along the road he stopped suddenly and bent double and – cried, if that's the word. He wept. I don't know how to say what it sounded like, though. At first I thought it was like an animal, just one long sound tearing up out of his belly. Then I thought it's the noise Adam might have made when he first had breath pushed into him and had to push it out again. Then I thought, it's the noise a dead man waking up would make, starting to breathe again.

He wept.

[*Stands, pause.*]

Doesn't tell you anything, that. You know – well, maybe you don't, you're lucky if you don't – you know what it sounds like when someone hasn't cried for years and it's kind of sucked up out of them? Only this was as if you were hearing weeping for the first time. As if it was being sucked up out of the ground or under the ground.

Everybody was quiet for a minute. Then I heard a bit of whispering and a laugh or two. He didn't look up or round. Then he straightened up and walked on. I could see her pointing to the grave.

He stopped again. There was quite a lot of noise by this time, but I could just hear him, whispering the dead boy's name. Then just, "Come." Like that, flat, short, dropping like a stone on the dust. "Lazarus, come forth." I can't remember if it was loud or quiet or what. It just dropped there.

SECOND VOICE

[*She gets up and walks towards the THIRD VOICE.*]

You hear about noises starting a landslide, don't you? One stone drops and then the hillside starts moving?

They'd moved the grave slab aside – lots of frowning and complaining over that, and it was there, balanced against the hillside, and it started shaking, just like him, he was still shivering, and then it fell over and slammed on the dry rocks.

[*Quietly.*] And he came to him. [*Pause; she speaks with difficulty.*] He came to him, and he said a strange thing, he said, "Let him go." He was very still now, he'd stopped shivering. They were both very still, and I thought, "Things come to him when he calls." [*Still laboured, feeling for words.*] The stone plug comes out of the grave hole, the breath comes to him – from the, from the end of the earth and he breathes it into the grave [*Faster.*] and the dead bodies come to him and the words come to him out of the dead bodies and, and – [*She grasps the sleeve of the first speaker.*]

[*Lets go, moves away*.] When the stone fell over, I thought it was a storm starting. And sure enough the rain suddenly came up and we were all running back indoors, with all those folk who'd turned up to see him not sure what they'd seen.

FIRST VOICE

[*Looks/moves toward SECOND VOICE.*]

I had a nightmare after that time looking through my aunt's stuff. I'd been to her funeral too, and I was back there in church looking at the coffin, and I went up to it and the lid started slipping off and I could see her face moving, like it was starting to breathe again, her mouth opening. And I was scared out of my mind that she'd – say something. Or that when she opened her mouth there'd be something inside it that I couldn't bear to see. There was a noise like rain beginning to hiss on a pavement when it starts to pour down, hissing getting louder and louder, more like a steam engine after a bit, and then the lid of the coffin just slid on the floor, a big loud wooden sound, and I sort of panicked and knocked the whole coffin over and it fell off the stand thing and clattered and echoed, and I woke up sweating like a pig. I realised it was a thunderstorm starting outside. Of course.

THIRD VOICE

[*Abstracted, to herself at first.*]

The rain came stabbing down. Washing the rocks, leaping off the rocks, white limestone turning black. I stood there for a long time. I felt my mind was like the rocks, soaked and streaming and turning dark. I am the Life, he said.

The rain strips the earth away and what's left is the rock. When he...when he wept, something, I don't know, something stripped the covers away and what's left is the life. Whatever's alive underneath it all. And you stand there, streaming with the darkness pouring over you, and he says, I'm what's left. You may go away, I won't. The water keeps on coming.

FIRST VOICE

[*Wanders towards audience.*]

Someone just back from a trip to China said he'd been to some kind of cultural event and they had this wooden gong. You think, "Wooden gongs?" He tried to describe it; he said it's like a hollow clap, you feel the emptiness all round; it sort of clears a space in your brain. I thought of that when I tried to think about this nightmare and the sound of falling boxes upstairs and the...the words I'd read. The sound before the rain comes and streams down the windows, and then you can see what you didn't see before. The Word was with God and the Word was God. Then the rain comes.

Sounds bloody daft like that, doesn't it? But I had this picture in my head, water scouring off the soil and the rock coming through. And all those big plain words just sitting there; only not rocks but more like – what? Some big patient animal, something alive. Like you think you're looking at a rock in the sea or a mound of earth in a wood and suddenly you notice it's looking at you. [*Sits.*] Something alive. The life that's left.

SECOND VOICE

It was so strange later on. Serving food to a table of silent faces. Because no one had anything to say. How could they?

We sat and listened to the rain. We listened to the rain. It was a long time. After a while, you could feel people settling back, as if all there ever was to do was listen to the rain. He was lying on his elbow, very pale, and his breath seemed to be coming slowly, and his eyes kept meeting Lazarus's eyes, as if he knew Lazarus knew something and knew he couldn't say it, and only the two of them would understand if he ever opened his mouth. I think – I think we were afraid at the thought he'd open his mouth...that either of them would open their mouths. Rain and the sounds of laboured breath and silence. Sometimes the big wooden noises overhead and the sudden light. [*Slowly moving towards audience.*] And when the rain stopped at last, he got up slowly and smiled at us all and said it was better for him to go away. And he went away.

FIRST VOICE

"I am the life." I'm what's alive here. That's what I was hearing. The hollow clap, then the rain, the flood. Words heavy enough to splinter the floor of the sky. Or whatever. You run out of things to say, you want to go back to the beginning, before....

SECOND VOICE

[*Pacing.*]

He never asked me if I wanted Lazarus back. Never asked Lazarus, if it comes to that. You think about it, and why would you want to come back? [*Still for a moment.*] No, that's not right, though, it's more that – well, you think the best thing is to sort of rest, really, specially when you think about what people go through. What Lazarus went through. No, he never asked. Like he couldn't *ask* permission to be – what he is. Whatever he is. So he weeps. It rains. The thunder makes great hollow noises. The words tumble over and roll downhill, lie around in the wet.

THIRD VOICE

[*Moving towards SECOND VOICE.*]

There they lie. I climb over them, I look to see if you can build something out of them. My fingers slip off them. [*Turns away then round to audience; pause.*] Even the world itself could not contain the books that should be written.

[*Silence: the three speakers stand still, looking at each other. Then the recorded voice again, reading "I am the Resurrection and the life." Pause. A wooden gong struck three times.*]

Acknowledgments

Shakeshafte had its first performance at the Dylan Thomas Theatre in Swansea in July 2016, and I want to acknowledge the generous enthusiasm of the Swansea Little Theatre in taking this on: special thanks to Dreena Morgan-Harvey, Chair of the Board of Swansea Little Theatre, and John Rhys Thomas, who did such a wonderful, thoughtful, and imaginative job of producing. Watching this was a great help to me in thinking through some possible revisions. I am also very grateful to Greg Garrett, Salley Vickers, James Roose-Evans, and Pip Williams for comments.

An earlier version of the text appeared in the special issue of *Critical Survey* (vol. 25.3, 2013) on "Creating Shakespeare," and in Katherine Scheil and Graham Holderness, eds., *Shakespeare and Biography*, New York/Oxford: Berghahn, 2020.

Valerie Doulton of the Live Literature Company arranged a rehearsed reading of *The Flat Roof of the World* in London in 2019; my thanks to her and to all who took part. Once again, this was an opportunity to think harder about what would and would not work dramatically, and helped me rework the balance of the play. Pip Williams pressed me about where the centre of gravity was for the whole piece; Rachel Mann helped me think through the moral risks for a male writer of trying to find a voice for a woman who has experienced abuse, as well as pointing out how easily descriptions of the trenches of the First World War could fall into cliché. I am very grateful to these early readers, and also to Greg Garrett and Kate Banks for their supportive response.

In 2010, Josie Rourke, then Director of the Bush Theatre in London, invited a number of writers to collaborate in a project entitled *Sixty Six Books*, designed to commemorate the fourth centenary of the King James Bible in 2011 – sixty six short plays loosely connected with the books of the Bible. *Lazarus* is my contribution to this project, and it was performed at the Bush Theatre and also in Westminster Abbey in 2011. Warmest thanks to Josie for the invitation and for her direction of the play. The text was published in *Sixty Six Books: 21st Century Writers Speak to the King James Bible*, London: Oberon Books 2012.

This book was set in Sabon, designed by the German typographer and book designer, Jan Tschichold, and released in 1967. Tschichold was inspired to design Sabon after encountering a sixteenth-century specimen sheet produced by the legendary printer and typographer, Claude Garamond (1480–1561). The typeface is named after one of Garamond's students and colleagues, Jacques Sabon (1535–ca. 1580–90).

This book was designed by Timothy R. Botts, Ian Creeger, and Gregory Wolfe. It was published in hardcover, paperback, and electronic formats by Slant Books, Seattle, Washington.

The lettering on the cover is by Timothy R. Botts, based on the style employed by the Anglo-Welsh artist and poet, David Jones.